D0152271

DISCARD

Rights of Students,
Second Edition

Rights of Students, Second Edition

David L. Hudson Jr.

SERIES EDITOR
Alan Marzilli, M.A., J.D.

An imprint of Infobase Publishing

Rights of Students

Chelsea House
An imprint of Infobase Publishing
132 West 31st Street
New York, NY 10001

Library of Congress Cataloging-in-Publication Data
Hudson, David L., 1969–
  Rights of students / by David L. Hudson, Jr. — 2nd ed.
  p. cm. — (Point/counterpoint)
  Includes bibliographical references and index.
  ISBN 978-1-60413-692-0 (hardcover)
  1. Students—Legal status, laws, etc.—United States—Juvenile literature. 2. School discipline—Law and legislation—United States—Juvenile literature. I. Title. II. Series.

  KF4150.H83 2010
  344.73'0793—dc22

                              2009051402

Chelsea House books are available at special discounts when purchased in bulk quantities for businesses, associations, institutions, or sales promotions. Please call our Special Sales Department in New York at (212) 967-8800 or (800) 322-8755.

You can find Chelsea House on the World Wide Web at http://www.chelseahouse.com.

Text design by Keith Trego
Cover design by Alicia Post
Composition by EJB Publishing Services
Cover printed by Bang Printing, Brainerd, MN
Book printed and bound by Bang Printing, Brainerd, MN
Date printed: October 2010
Printed in the United States of America

10 9 8 7 6 5 4 3 2 1

This book is printed on acid-free paper.

All links and Web addresses were checked and verified to be correct at the time of publication. Because of the dynamic nature of the Web, some addresses and links may have changed since publication and may no longer be valid.

FOREWORD ▐▐▐▐▷

Alan Marzilli, M.A., J.D.
Birmingham, Alabama

The POINT/COUNTERPOINT series offers the reader a greater understanding of some of the most controversial issues in contemporary
American society—issues such as capital punishment, immigration,
gay rights, and gun control. We have looked for the most contemporary issues and have included topics—such as the controversies
surrounding "blogging"—that we could not have imagined when the
series began.

In each volume, the author has selected an issue of particular
importance and set out some of the key arguments on both sides of the
issue. Why study both sides of the debate? Maybe you have yet to make
up your mind on an issue, and the arguments presented in the book
will help you to form an opinion. More likely, however, you will already
have an opinion on many of the issues covered by the series. There is
always the chance that you will change your opinion after reading the
arguments for the other side. But even if you are firmly committed to
an issue—for example, school prayer or animal rights—reading both
sides of the argument will help you to become a more effective advocate for your cause. By gaining an understanding of opposing arguments, you can develop answers to those arguments.

Perhaps more importantly, listening to the other side sometimes
helps you see your opponent's arguments in a more human way. For
example, Sister Helen Prejean, one of the nation's most visible opponents of capital punishment, has been deeply affected by her interac-
tions with the families of murder victims. By seeing the families' grief
and pain, she understands much better why people support the death
penalty, and she is able to carry out her advocacy with a greater sensi-
tivity to the needs and beliefs of death penalty supporters.

The books in the series include numerous features that help the
reader to gain a greater understanding of the issues. Real-life examples
illustrate the human side of the issues. Each chapter also includes
excerpts from relevant laws, court cases, and other material, which
provide a better foundation for understanding the arguments. The

volumes contain citations to relevant sources of law and information, and an appendix guides the reader through the basics of legal research, both on the Internet and in the library. Today, through free Web sites, it is easy to access legal documents, and these books might give you ideas for your own research.

Studying the issues covered by the POINT/COUNTERPOINT series is more than an academic activity. The issues described in the books affect all of us as citizens. They are the issues that today's leaders debate and tomorrow's leaders will decide. While all of the issues covered in the POINT/COUNTERPOINT series are controversial today, and will remain so for the foreseeable future, it is entirely possible that the reader might one day play a central role in resolving the debate. Today it might seem that some debates—such as capital punishment and abortion—will never be resolved.

However, our nation's history is full of debates that seemed as though they never would be resolved, and many of the issues are now well settled—at least on the surface. In the nineteenth century, abolitionists met with widespread resistance to their efforts to end slavery. Ultimately, the controversy threatened the union, leading to the Civil War between the northern and southern states. Today, while a public debate over the merits of slavery would be unthinkable, racism persists in many aspects of society.

Similarly, today nobody questions women's right to vote. Yet at the beginning of the twentieth century, suffragists fought public battles for women's voting rights, and it was not until the passage of the Nineteenth Amendment in 1920 that the legal right of women to vote was established nationwide.

What makes an issue controversial? Often, controversies arise when most people agree that there is a problem but disagree about the best way to solve it. There is little argument that poverty is a major problem in the United States, especially in inner cities and rural areas. Yet, people disagree vehemently about the best way to address the problem. To some, the answer is social programs, such as welfare, food stamps, and public housing. However, many argue that such subsidies encourage dependence on government benefits while unfairly penalizing those who work and pay taxes, and that the real solution is to require people to support themselves.

American society is in a constant state of change, and sometimes modern practices clash with what many consider to be "traditional values," which are often rooted in conservative political views or religious beliefs. Many blame high crime rates, and problems such as poverty, illiteracy, and drug use on the breakdown of the traditional family structure of a married mother and father raising their children. Since the "sexual revolution" of the 1960s and 1970s, sparked in part by the widespread availability of the birth control pill, marriage rates have declined, and the number of children born outside of marriage has increased. The sexual revolution led to controversies over birth control, sex education, and other issues, most prominently abortion. Similarly, the gay rights movement has been challenged as a threat to traditional values. While many gay men and lesbians want to have the same right to marry and raise families as heterosexuals, many politicians and others have challenged gay marriage and adoption as a threat to American society.

Sometimes, new technology raises issues that we have never faced before, and society disagrees about the best solution. Are people free to swap music online, or does this violate the copyright laws that protect songwriters and musicians' ownership of the music that they create? Should scientists use "genetic engineering" to create new crops that are resistant to disease and pests and produce more food, or is it too risky to use a laboratory to create plants that nature never intended? Modern medicine has continued to increase the average lifespan—which is now 77 years, up from under 50 years at the beginning of the twentieth century—but many people are now choosing to die in comfort rather than living with painful ailments in their later years. For doctors, this presents an ethical dilemma: should they allow their patients to die? Should they assist patients in ending their own lives painlessly?

Perhaps the most controversial issues are those that implicate a Constitutional right. The Bill of Rights—the first 10 Amendments to the U.S. Constitution—spells out some of the most fundamental rights that distinguish our democracy from other nations with fewer freedoms. However, the sparsely worded document is open to interpretation, with each side saying that the Constitution is on their side. The Bill of Rights was meant to protect individual liberties; however, the needs of some individuals clash with society's needs. Thus, the Constitution often serves as a battleground between individuals and government officials seeking to protect society in some way. The First Amendment's guarantee of "freedom of speech" leads to some very difficult questions. Some forms of expression—such as burning an American flag—lead to public outrage, but are protected by the First Amendment. Other types of expression that most people find objectionable—such as child pornography—are not protected by the Constitution. The question is not only where to draw the line, but whether drawing lines around constitutional rights threatens our liberty.

The Bill of Rights raises many other questions about individual rights and societal "good." Is a prayer before a high school football game an "establishment of religion" prohibited by the First Amendment? Does the Second Amendment's promise of "the right to bear arms" include concealed handguns? Does stopping and frisking someone standing on a known drug corner constitute "unreasonable search and seizure" in violation of the Fourth Amendment? Although the U.S. Supreme Court has the ultimate authority in interpreting the U.S. Constitution, its answers do not always satisfy the public. When a group of nine people—sometimes by a five-to-four vote—makes a decision that affects hundreds of millions of others, public outcry can be expected. For example, the Supreme Court's 1973 ruling in *Roe v. Wade* that abortion is protected by the Constitution did little to quell the debate over abortion.

Whatever the root of the controversy, the books in the POINT/ COUNTERPOINT series seek to explain to the reader the origins of the debate, the current state of the law, and the arguments on either side of the debate. Our hope in creating this series is that readers will be better informed about the issues facing not only our politicians, but all of our nation's citizens, and become more actively involved in resolving these debates, as voters, concerned citizens, journalists, or maybe even elected officials.

Although the nation's classrooms are often called "laboratories for democracy," school officials have much more ability to regulate conduct than other government officials. As the U.S. Supreme Court noted in upholding the rights of students to protest the Vietnam War, students do not shed their constitutional rights at the schoolhouse gate. However, the Court has ruled on numerous occasions that students have fewer rights in school than outside of the school environment. In recent years, schools have been enacting an increasing number of restrictions to deal with the problems of gangs, drugs, and inappropriate sexual behavior. Since the first edition of this book was published in 2004, the problem of "cyberbullying"—using e-mail, Web sites, and social networks to antagonize peers—has grabbed headlines. Many parents and school officials argue that incidents such as school shootings, sexual assaults, and suicides underscore the need for tighter restrictions on students. Many students, however, with the support of parents and civil liberties groups, argue that restrictions on speech and other forms of expression—such as hairstyles and clothing—set a dangerous precedent. This volume examines both sides of controversial issues such as "zero tolerance" policies, searches of students, drug testing, and dress codes.

Constitutional Rights in School

Students attend school to learn how to become fully functioning citizens in our constitutional democracy. The primary role of school administrators is to ensure that students receive a quality education that will prepare them for the rest of their lives. For this reason, school officials must see to it that students have a safe school environment in which to learn. School officials stand *in loco parentis* (in the place of parents) to a certain extent during the school day. This means that school officials exercise a great deal of control over students and their behavior. The power of public school officials over students, however, is not absolute. Public schools, as arms of the government, are subject to the Bill of Rights and the Fourteenth Amendment. These constitutional provisions guarantee that all citizens, including public school students, receive protection of their individual liberties from governmental interference.

The Bill of Rights

The Bill of Rights, which consists of the first 10 amendments to the U.S. Constitution, declares that individuals normally cannot legally be punished for criticizing public officials, practicing a certain religion, or peacefully assembling in support of a cause. The Bill of Rights prevents government officials from ransacking private homes for no legitimate reason, imprisoning persons for lengthy periods of time without a fair and impartial trial, or subjecting people to cruel and unusual punishment.

The Bill of Rights serves as the blueprint for Americans' personal liberty. The First Amendment provides protections for freedom of religion, speech, press, assembly, and petition. The Fourth Amendment provides that governmental officials cannot conduct unreasonable searches and seizures. The Eighth Amendment prevents government officials from inflicting cruel and unusual punishment. When originally adopted in 1791, the Bill of Rights only applied to protect people from the federal government. In 1868, however, the states ratified the Fourteenth Amendment, which amended the Constitution to provide that states may not infringe on individuals' rights to "life, liberty or property without due process of law." Throughout much of the twentieth century, the U.S. Supreme Court interpreted the Fourteenth Amendment to extend the vast majority of the protections of the Bill of Rights to the states as well as the federal government.

Public school administrators, as state officials, must act according to the dictates of the U.S. Constitution. This means that public school students do not forfeit all of their constitutional rights when they attend school. The U.S. Supreme Court ruled in the 1943 case *West Virginia Board of Education v. Barnette* that school officials violated the First and Fourteenth amendments when they punished students and their parents for the students' refusal to salute the American flag in school. Justice Robert Jackson wrote for the Court:

The Fourteenth Amendment, as now applied to the States, protects the citizen against the State itself and all of its creatures—Boards of Education not excepted. These have, of course, important, delicate, and highly discretionary functions, but none that they may not perform within the limits of the Bill of Rights. That they are educating the young for citizenship is reason for scrupulous protection of Constitutional freedoms of the individual, if we are not to strangle the free mind at its source and teach youth to discount important principles of our government as mere platitudes.[1]

The Bill of Rights in Public Schools

This landmark ruling ensured that students possessed some level of constitutional rights even when they were attending public schools. Previously, school officials had had the right to act with virtual impunity in dealing with students under their control. Legal commentator Stuart Leviton explains that "the Court's defense of students' rights [in *Barnette*] and its opposition to coercive tactics foster a view of the Constitution as a baseline, deviations below which we will not tolerate and above which we constantly strive."[2]

The courts, however, have determined that public school students, the vast majority of whom are minors, do *not* retain the full level of rights that adults enjoy in nonschool settings. In fact, minors do not have the same level of rights as adults whether they are in school or not. For instance, people do not acquire the right to vote until they reach the age of majority, usually eighteen. Second, students receive even fewer rights while they are in school than they have outside of school, because school officials wield great power to help them provide a safe learning environment.

The question remains: What level of rights do young people possess when they attend public schools? Students possess some degree of free speech rights, but certainly they are not permitted to say anything they want. Students retain some level of Fourth Amendment rights, but school officials may sometimes conduct searches of a student's person and belongings on school grounds.

In its 1969 decision *Tinker v. Des Moines Independent Community School District*, the U.S. Supreme Court determined that students do not lose their First Amendment rights at school. The Court explained: "School officials do not possess absolute authority over their students. Students in school as well as out of school are 'persons' under our Constitution. They are possessed of fundamental rights which the State must respect, just as they themselves must respect their obligations to the State."[3]

The Court determined that school officials violated the First Amendment rights of several junior high and high school students when they suspended them for wearing black armbands to school to protest U.S. involvement in the Vietnam War. The *Tinker* case is seen as the high-water mark of student constitutional rights. The case established a constitutional test—the substantial disruption test—that school officials must meet before they infringe upon student rights.

Decades later, however, public school students do not seem to possess the same level of rights they had during the *Tinker* era. Dan Johnston, the attorney who successfully argued the *Tinker* case for the students, believes the current U.S. Supreme Court would decide the case differently today: "The real question now is whether the present-day Supreme Court would reach the same decision. I think the answer is probably not."[4]

Thirty years after *Tinker*, public school officials in Louisiana and Texas suspended students for wearing black armbands to school. Jennifer Boccia, a student in Texas, was suspended along with some of her classmates when they wore black armbands to mourn the victims of the school shooting at Columbine High School in Littleton, Colorado, and to protest more restrictive school policies after Columbine.[5]

Another student, Jennifer Roe from Louisiana, was suspended for wearing a black armband to protest the adoption of a restrictive policy on student dress. When she informed her school principal that the *Tinker* case protected her First Amendment rights, the principal allegedly said that he and the school board did not care about the *Tinker* case.[6] Even more recently, in 2006, a group of students in Arkansas wore black armbands to protest the adoption of a mandatory school uniform policy. The school officials suspended the students for wearing the black armbands. The students successfully sued in federal court to vindicate their rights under Tinker.[7]

Students today live in a world filled with violent and sexual imagery. Drugs and weapons have become all too common in the lives of many young people. Many students have faced violence, or at least feared violence, during the school day. Cyberbullying—harassment using e-mail, social networking sites, or other online tools—has become a major issue in and out of schools. It has become enough of an issue that the U.S. Congress is holding hearings to determine whether to pass federal legislation that would criminalize at least some forms of cyberbullying. School officials understandably must take measures to ensure the safety of students. They must take seriously the issue of even violent-themed student writing.

Summary

The issue of student rights is intimately wrapped up in this maelstrom of controversy over violence, school safety, and zero tolerance. The challenge for school administrators, students, parents, and other interested citizens is to find a way to balance student rights and school safety, to balance rights with responsibilities.

This book examines three hot button issues in the public schools: zero tolerance policies, search and seizure issues, and student dress. The issue of zero tolerance presents intriguing questions of balancing student rights with school discipline. Proponents contend zero tolerance policies are necessary in a post-Columbine environment, while opponents counter that zero tolerance policies result in overreaction and the violation of student rights.

Similarly, search and seizure questions abound in the public schools. Some contend that school officials must possess broad authority to search students' lockers, desks, and persons in order to provide a safe learning environment. Critics argue that school officials often violate the Fourth Amendment of the Constitution, particularly when they engage in invasive strip searches and act without suspicion that a particular student has engaged in wrongdoing.

Finally, the book examines the issue of student dress codes and uniforms. Supporters argue that dress codes and uniforms create an environment more suited to learning, while detractors counter that many such policies stifle individual creativity and silence student expression.

Zero Tolerance Policies Work

"Zero Tolerance" is a common sense policy. Why does anybody need to have a gun in school? That's why this order directs the Secretary of Education to withhold funding the states that don't comply with the law. Young people simply should not have to live in fear of young criminals who carry guns to schools.
—President Bill Clinton, October 22, 1994[1]

Public schools face a litany of safety problems, from the discharge of weapons to illegal drug consumption to sexual harassment and bullying. In 1978, the Safe School Study Report presented to the U.S. Congress showed the prevalence of crime in public schools. The study found that thousands of students and teachers were assaulted each year and nearly half a million students felt afraid at school.[2] In 1985, the U.S. Supreme Court recognized the problem of crime in schools: "[M]aintaining order in the classroom has never been easy, but in recent years, school disorder has often taken particularly ugly forms: drug use and violent crime in the schools have become major social problems."[3]

Too many students are exposed to illegal drugs and weapons at school. During a spate of fatal school shootings, school officials realize that they sometimes must take drastic measures to ensure that this disturbing pattern does not continue. One way to send the message to students is to enact get-tough disciplinary measures that send a clear signal that unlawful student behavior will not be tolerated. Zero tolerance policies are an outgrowth of this thinking.

Zero tolerance is the term for policies based on the premise that violence and threats of violence will not be accepted in any form. Under these policies, students will be punished swiftly and severely for bringing weapons or drugs to school. Many zero tolerance programs extend beyond weapons and guns, though. A whole range of behavior may run afoul of zero tolerance policies, including sexual harassment, bullying, hate speech, and other disruptive behavior. For instance, Louisiana law empowers local school boards to adopt zero tolerance policies for fighting.[4] A school safety counselor recommends to parents that they "urge school officials to establish a 'zero tolerance' policy regarding any verbal or written remarks made by students who insinuate acts of violence, to include an immediate and aggressive intervention approach."[5]

Many trace the origin of the term *zero tolerance* to a federal government policy against illegal drugs in the 1980s. U.S. Attorney Peter Nunez used the term to describe a program of impounding seagoing vessels carrying illegal drugs.[6] In 1994, the federal government passed the Gun-Free Schools Act. This law made federal funds contingent on a state's passing a zero tolerance law providing for a one-year expulsion of any student caught with a weapon on school grounds.

This law led every state in the nation to pass a similar gun-free school act. State zero tolerance laws vary widely. Some apply

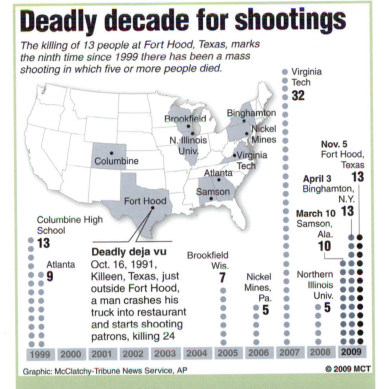

Deadly decade for shootings

The killing of 13 people at Fort Hood, Texas, marks the ninth time since 1999 there has been a mass shooting in which five or more people died.

Virginia Tech
32

Brookfield

Binghamton

N. Illinois Univ.

Nickel Mines

Columbine

Virginia Tech

Atlanta

Samson

Fort Hood

Columbine High School
13

Atlanta
9

Deadly deja vu
Oct. 16, 1991, Killeen, Texas, just outside Fort Hood, a man crashes his truck into restaurant and starts shooting patrons, killing 24

Brookfield Wis.
7

Nickel Mines, Pa.
5

Nov. 5
Fort Hood, Texas

April 3   **13**
Binghamton, N.Y.

March 10 **13**
Samson, Ala.
10

Northern Illinois Univ.
5

| 1999 | 2000 | 2001 | 2002 | 2003 | 2004 | 2005 | 2006 | 2007 | 2008 | 2009 |

Graphic: McClatchy-Tribune News Service, AP   © 2009 MCT

This map and timeline depicts the largest mass shootings in the United States since the Columbine High School shooting in 1999. In a violent society, fears of more mass shootings have prompted many school officials to implement tough regulations on their students.

to weapons. Others apply to both drugs and weapons. Still others apply to fighting and other forms of disruptive behavior.

Zero tolerance policies reduce school violence.

Zero tolerance policies help schools become safer by cracking down on weapons and drugs. Many school officials say that these policies have helped in their schools. "Now that the students are more carefully controlled, there are decidedly fewer opportunities for violence," said one middle school principal.[7] A school board attorney for a Florida county high school district indicates that since the advent of the zero tolerance policy, alcohol offenses have dropped dramatically.

A national poll of 1,350 elementary school principals showed that 90 percent of them said that zero tolerance policies for weapons, harassment, and drugs were essential for school safety.[8] A Gallup poll in 1997 of more than 1,100 adults showed that 86 percent favored a zero tolerance policy for drug and alcohol violations and 93 percent favored such a policy for weapons violations.[9]

Sandra Feldman, president of the American Federation of Teachers, supports zero tolerance policies as a method of bringing about higher standards in student behavior. "Zero tolerance policies work," she says. "Where they have been appropriately

THE LETTER OF THE LAW

Louisiana Zero Tolerance Law for Public Schools La. Rev. Stat. Ann. 17: 416.16

The following is an excerpt from Louisiana's zero tolerance law:

> Any city, parish, or other local public school board may adopt and implement a *zero tolerance* policy for fighting in the schools under its jurisdiction. Such policy may include a requirement that a student who is disciplined pursuant to the policy and such student's parent or parents shall attend a conflict resolution class or classes and may include provisions for the school board to take appropriate action, as determined by the board, against any student or parent who fails to comply with the class attendance requirement. Such classes may be provided by the school board or other appropriate provider as determined by the board. Any city, parish, or other local public school board may charge a fee for such attendance in an amount as may be determined by the board. However, such fee amount shall not exceed one hundred dollars.

The rate of student deaths has dropped since the mid-1990s when school officials began implementing zero tolerance policies.

applied to serious offenses, there have been fewer incidents of violence and disruption."[10]

Critics have emphasized a few instances of overreaction in which students are expelled or suspended for bringing nail clippers to class or using a rubber band to shoot a paper clip. Although there have been a few instances of draconian punishments, zero tolerance policies have proven to be successful. "The vast majority of school officials apply zero-tolerance policies very well," says Ron Stephens, executive director of the National School Safety Center.[11]

Former president Bill Clinton summed up many people's feelings about the need for zero tolerance when he said, "We cannot operate in a country where children are afraid and cannot feel, much less think. You cannot learn in that kind of atmosphere."[12] Zero tolerance policies help ensure that students can learn in safe educational environments.

Most zero tolerance policies are constitutional.

School officials must have authority to make day-to-day discipline decisions free from judicial interference. School officials, not federal judges who are removed from the realities of the school environment, are in the best position to determine punishment decisions for students. The job of school administrators is a daunting one, and many courts are hesitant to second-guess the decisions of school officials, especially in the area of school safety.

School officials have the discretion to enforce zero tolerance policies as long as they do not violate students' due process rights. Due process of law is an important legal concept that generally means people must be informed of any charges they face. Students do possess certain due process rights at school. For example, students must receive notice of any charges being made against them and must be allowed some sort of hearing in which they can present their side of the story. Zero tolerance policies should provide some sort of review mechanism in which students can challenge the charges they face.

Even punishments that may seem unfair do not necessarily violate the Constitution. A prime example is the case of *Ratner v. Loudoun County Public Schools*.[13] In this decision, 13-year-old Benjamin Ratner was expelled from middle school for taking a knife away from another student who said she was suicidal. The problem was that Ratner did not tell school officials about the knife. The school principal acknowledged that Ratner believed he had acted in his classmate's best interests and did not intend to harm anyone with the knife. The court of appeals wrote: "However harsh the result in this case, the federal courts are not properly called upon to judge the wisdom of a zero tolerance policy of the sort alleged to be in place at Blue Ridge Middle School or of its application to Ratner."[14]

Most courts have upheld state laws providing for stiff penalties for students who bring weapons to schools. In *Cathe A. v. Doddridge County Board of Education*, the West Virginia Supreme Court ruled that a state zero tolerance law that called for a 12-month expulsion was constitutional. A student challenged the law, arguing that it was unconstitutional because the state constitution said education was a fundamental right. The state supreme court, however, ruled that the state *could* infringe on this fundamental right in order to ensure its compelling interest in safe and secure schools. The 12-month penalty served as an effective deterrent to prevent students from bringing weapons to school.[15]

Zero tolerance policies are also constitutional as applied to threatening, profane, or even inappropriate speech. For example, a federal appeals court ruled that a school could suspend a kindergarten student for violating a zero tolerance policy against threatening speech. The student said, "I'm going to shoot you," while playing a game of cops and robbers with friends. This incident took place shortly after another student had said he intended to shoot a teacher. The court wrote that school officials could reasonably believe they were acting within the scope of their permissible authority in deciding that the use of threatening language at school undermines the school's basic educational mission, particularly because the incident was only two weeks after the widely reported fatal shooting of a six-year-old child by another six-year-old child at an elementary school in Flint, Michigan.[16] A federal district court upheld a school district's zero tolerance policy against the use of profane or inappropriate language on school grounds. A student received a suspension after uttering profanity in the principal's office upon reading a note from her mother about riding the bus home. The court reasoned that school officials have the ability to regulate indecent language in schools.[17]

The supreme court of Indiana upheld a suspension of a student who was found to possess a small amount of marijuana in his pickup truck on school grounds. The student committed the offense only three days before the end of the fall semester. School officials suspended the student for the rest of the fall semester and the entire spring semester. Although the student challenged the school board's decision in court, the state's supreme court upheld the punishment, reasoning that school officials had the power to make such a decision.

Unless the decision is arbitrary or capricious, the court determined, school officials can punish students under a zero tolerance policy for drugs. "Whether the school board should re-examine its policy is not a matter for the courts to decide," Indiana's supreme court wrote.[18]

Summary

Media headlines too often focus on the occasional harsh application of zero tolerance policies. Most systems are based on the realization that weapons, drugs, threats of violence, and other disruptive behavior can create an unsafe environment that is not conducive to learning. If there is an occasional punishment that is too harsh, this can be remedied on a case-by-case basis in the courts.

Some people argue that zero tolerance policies have not reduced school violence and do not solve deeper societal problems. These critics charge that violence is endemic in American society. This may be true, but zero tolerance policies are still worthwhile. As one commentator has written:

> Whether effective or not, zero-tolerance policies send the American public the message that schools are taking positive, aggressive action to address a situation that is perceived to be a real and present danger for schools and children. The media coverage given to recent incidents of school violence only galvanizes public opinion in favor of zero-tolerance and harsh penalties for students who bring weapons to school.[19]

Fundamentally, zero tolerance policies send a clear message to students that there are consequences for breaking the rules. Zero tolerance tells students that violence and threats of violence are unacceptable in a civilized society. Students possess many rights and freedoms under the U.S. Constitution, but with those rights come responsibilities. Zero tolerance policies that are properly drafted and respect due process rights protect students, teachers, and school employees and are an effective way to make schools safer.

Zero Tolerance Policies Are Unfair

The push for zero tolerance laws has led to inconsistent results, inappropriately extreme punishments for minor offenses, and the marginalization of many minority students. Granted, school officials need authority to make the learning environment safe. But inflexible, one-size-fits-all prison-style policies are not the answer. Minor offenses should not be punished in the same way as major infractions. A student who brings a loaded gun to school deserves severe punishment, probably expulsion. But students who bring, for example, a squirt gun or a toy gun should not face the same punishment.

There have been numerous egregious examples of overreaction by school officials. In Fort Myers, Florida, an honor student was suspended for five days for having a steak knife in the back of his car. In Pennsylvania, a kindergartener was suspended for wearing a five-inch plastic ax to a Halloween party in his class.

In Chicago, a high school student was suspended for shooting a paper clip with a rubber band that hit a school cafeteria worker. A sixth grader in the state of Washington was expelled when a squirt gun fell out of his backpack.[1] One commentator summarizes: "However well-meaning those policies have been, the pages of national newspapers have been littered with the wreckage of young lives changed, perhaps irrevocably, by policies whose primary aim is to send a message to more serious offenders."[2]

Unfortunately, the adoption of zero tolerance policies has led to a marked increase of school expulsions and suspensions. The result of these policies is that "thousands of students are now routinely excluded from school each year for relatively innocuous or unintentional actions that are neither violent nor dangerous."[3] Such unfairness led the American Bar Association (ABA), the leading organization of lawyers in the United States, to call for an end to inflexible zero tolerance policies. The ABA adopted a resolution, stating that it "opposes, in principle, 'zero tolerance' policies that have a discriminatory effect, or mandate either expulsion or referral of students to juvenile or criminal court, without regard to the circumstances or nature of the offense or the student's history."[4]

Zero tolerance policies do not lead to safer schools.

There is little, if any, evidence that the adoption of zero tolerance policies have made schools safer. Russell Skiba of the Indiana University School of Education and Kimberly Knesting from the University of Wisconsin–Eau Claire wrote that "[d]espite more than ten years of implementation in school districts around the country, there is no convincing documentation that zero tolerance has in any way contributed to school safety or improved student behavior."[5]

In fact, some educational experts argue that zero tolerance policies may have the opposite effect. Education professor Ronnie Casella argued in *At Zero Tolerance* that "at the very best, zero tolerance may temporarily exclude from school a kid who is potentially violent, but, inevitably, that student will return and will do so with a vengeance."[6] Casella warned that inflexible punishment policies risk turning schools into prisons. These policies create a disconnection between students and teachers and run the risk of breaking bonds of communication and trust that foster safer schools. If students do not feel close to

Excerpt from the American Bar Association's Report on Zero Tolerance Policies

Public policy towards children has moved towards treating them more like adults and in ways that increasingly mimic the adult criminal justice system. The most recent version of this movement is so-called "zero tolerance" in schools, where theories of punishment that were once directed to adult criminals are now applied to first graders. . . .

While zero tolerance policies target the serious risk of students bringing guns to school, they also go after other weapons or anything—like a Swiss Army knife—that can be used as a weapon. Zero tolerance responds to student violence (covering a wide range of activities) or threats of violence. Zero tolerance is theoretically directed at students who misbehave intentionally, yet it also applies to those who misbehave as a result of emotional problems, or other disabilities, or who merely forget what is in their pocket after legitimate non-school activities. It treats alike first graders and twelfth graders.

Zero tolerance results in expulsion or suspension irrespective of any legitimate explanation. In many instances it also results in having the student arrested. . . .

Although few could quarrel with a policy of zero tolerance towards children who misbehave—adults who raise, teach or supervise children should react to misbehavior—their responses should be appropriate to the age, history and circumstances of the child as well as to the nature of the offense. Unfortunately, when it is examined closely, "zero tolerance" turns out to have very little to do with zero tolerance, and everything to do with one-size-fits-all mandatory punishment.

Source: American Bar Association, "ABA Zero Tolerance Policy." http://www.abanet.org/ crimjust/juvjus/zerotolreport.html.

their teachers, they are less likely to communicate meaningfully with them. This breakdown in communication could ultimately prove disastrous to school safety.

Rather than adopting inflexible, prison-style policies, school officials should put into effect flexible systems that carefully consider the punishment for particular offenses. Skiba and Knesting offer the following recommendations for schools with respect to school discipline and zero tolerance:

- Reserve zero tolerance disciplinary removals for only the most serious and severe of disruptive behaviors, such as weapon offenses, and define those behaviors explicitly.
- Replace one-size-fits-all disciplinary strategies with graduated systems of discipline, with consequences geared to the seriousness of the infraction.
- Expand the array of options available to schools for dealing with disruptive or violent behavior.
- Implement preventive measures that can improve school climate and reconnect alienated students.
- Evaluate all school-discipline or school-violence-prevention strategies to ensure that those strategies are truly having an impact on student behavior and school safety.[7]

Zero tolerance polices unfairly impact minority students.

Zero tolerance policies disparately impact minority students, particularly African Americans. For years, studies have shown racial differences in the imposition of school discipline. "The widespread use of zero-tolerance policies has exacerbated the racial gap in discipline," wrote commentators Judith A. Browne, Daniel J. Losen, and Johanna Wald in their article "Zero Tolerance, Unfair, With Little Recourse."[8] In Providence, Rhode Island, an African-American high school student faced expulsion for violating a zero tolerance policy on weapons after he pulled out a keychain knife to help his teacher remove a diskette from a school computer.

However, in one case from Vermont, a white high school student was exempted from punishment for bringing a loaded shotgun to school. His excuse was that it was hunting season. This disparity in treatment between the black and white youths is a disturbing pattern identified in numerous studies by researchers.[9]

A study conducted jointly by the Advancement Project and the Civil Rights Project at Harvard University found evidence of the "color of zero tolerance." The study found that schools with predominantly African-American or Latino students were more likely to have a zero tolerance policy. The study also found that African-American students were charged with violating the more subjective offenses, such as showing disrespect for authority or causing disturbances.[10]

School officials who discriminate based on race violate both the equal protection clause of the Fourteenth Amendment and Title VI of the Civil Rights Act of 1964. The Fourteenth Amendment was ratified in 1868 to protect recently freed

QUOTABLE

An Excerpt from *Opportunities Suspended: The Devastating Consequences of Zero Tolerance and School Discipline*

The continuing pattern of racial disparities in school discipline is an issue that cannot be ignored. Regardless of whether intentional discrimination is the cause of the disproportionate suspension and expulsion of black and Latino children, the statistics are quite troubling. More research is needed to determine the cause of the disparities. In addition, the Department of Education's Office for Civil Rights, which is entrusted with the enforcement of Title VI, should vigorously investigate these disparities. Our society cannot afford to leave any one segment of our population behind.

Source: http://www.civilrightsproject.ucla.edu/research/discipline/opport_suspended. php#fullreport.

African-American slaves from discrimination. Its equal protection clause now protects anyone who is the victim of racial discrimination. Fundamentally, it requires the federal, state, and local governments to treat all people equally, regardless of race. Title VI is a federal law that applies to all schools that receive federal funding. It, too, prohibits race discrimination.

Zero tolerance policies that result in disparate treatment and disparate impact can be challenged in court under Title VI. *Disparate treatment* refers to intentional discrimination based on race. *Disparate impact* refers to a seemingly neutral policy that results in an adverse effect upon a particular group.

Zero tolerance policies can violate the due process rights of students.

Public school students do not forfeit their constitutional rights when they pass through the schoolhouse doors. Among the rights they retain is the fundamental protection of due process. In *Goss v. Lopez*, the U.S. Supreme Court established that students facing suspensions have procedural due process rights, including notice of the charges and a hearing to present their own version of the events. According to the Court, "students facing suspension and the consequent interference with a protected property interest must be given *some* kind of notice and afforded *some* kind of hearing."[11] This is known as procedural due process. It ensures that an individual is entitled to a fair set of official legal procedures before being subject to serious discipline.

Due process also contains a second component, called substantive due process, which essentially means that government infringements of fundamental rights must not be irrational and arbitrary. That is, a school could not suspend or expel a student without a legitimate reason for doing so. Punishments must be rational and proportional to the violation.

Some zero tolerance policies run afoul of the requirements of due process. The U.S. Supreme Court in *Goss v. Lopez* wrote that "[the] very nature of due process negates any concept of inflexible procedures universally applicable to every imaginable situation."[12]

Several lower courts have determined that zero tolerance policies violated the due process rights of public school students. In *Lyons v. Penn Hills School District*, a Pennsylvania court determined that a school district violated the rights of a seventh grader who was expelled for bringing a Swiss Army knife to school. School officials contended that the knife was a weapon under the district's zero tolerance policy and that the offense merited a one-year suspension.

The Pennsylvania commonwealth court, however, ruled that the school officials' unwritten zero tolerance policy violated the state law that empowered school superintendents to "recommend modifications of such expulsion requirements for a student on a case-by-case basis." In other words, state law provided that schools had the authority to suspend students for a year for bringing weapons on school property, but the law also provided that schools adopt written policies and allow superintendents to modify punishments on an individual basis. The court concluded that the school board "exceeded its authority in adopting

FROM THE BENCH

Goss v. Lopez, 419 U.S. 565 (1975)

We do not believe that school authorities must be totally free from notice and hearing requirements if their schools are to operate with acceptable efficiency. Students facing temporary suspension have interests qualifying for protection of the Due Process Clause, and due process requires, in connection with a suspension of 10 days or less, that the student be given oral or written notice of the charges against him and, if he denies them, an explanation of the evidence the authorities have and an opportunity to present his side of the story. The Clause requires at least these rudimentary precautions against unfair or mistaken findings of misconduct and arbitrary exclusion from school.

its 'zero tolerance policy,' which denies the superintendent, the Board and the students the exercise of discretion specifically provided by . . . [state law] . . . and which frustrates the clear legislative intent that this statute not be blindly applied."[13]

A federal appeals court determined that Tennessee high school officials violated the substantive due process rights of a student who was suspended under a zero tolerance policy

FROM THE BENCH

Lyons v. Penn Hills School District, No. 723 A. 2d 1073 (Pa. Commonwealth 1999)

During the 1997–98 school year, twelve-year-old Adam Lyons was a seventh grade student at Linton Middle School. Lyons was an "A" student and a member of the chorus. On February 9, 1998, Lyons' instructor observed Lyons filing a fingernail with a miniature Swiss army knife he had found in a school hallway. The instructor requested Lyons to turn over the penknife and Lyons complied without incident. The knife was ultimately brought to the school's associate principal, who questioned Lyons about it. Lyons told the associate principal that he had found the knife and had intended to turn it over to his instructor. . . .

A hearing was held on February 23, 1998, before a Board-appointed hearing examiner. . . . The director of secondary education stated that the District does not permit weapons of any type on campus or at school functions. She testified that the knife in question constitutes a weapon under the District's "zero tolerance policy" and thus, a one-year suspension was warranted. She also stated that the disciplinary determination did not involve consideration of a student's record. . . .

The hearing examiner concluded that Lyons' possession of the penknife violated the District's discipline code and weapons policy. The hearing examiner opined that expulsion was a harsh result in this case, but concluded that he had no discretion to make an exception to the District's policy and had no alternative but to recommend expulsion for one year. The Board unanimously adopted the hearing examiner's recommendation and notified Lyons of its decision by letter dated March 11, 1998.

Lyons filed a timely appeal to the trial court, arguing that the District had violated his substantive and procedural due process rights. The trial court found for having a knife in his car. However, the student alleged that he had no knowledge that the knife was there, since the knife belonged to his friend. The U.S. Court of Appeals for the Sixth Circuit ruled in *Seal v. Morgan* that "suspending or expelling a student for weapons possession, even if the student did not knowingly possess any weapon, would not be rationally related to any legitimate state interest."[14] The court explained that "the

that, while the District's "zero tolerance policy" had been adopted by vote, it had never been reduced to writing. . . .

On appeal to this Court, the District . . . concedes that it has no written "zero tolerance policy." However, the District argues that Section 1317.2 of the School Code mandates that the Board expel a student who possesses a weapon on school property and that its policy comports with the act's requirements. . . .

The District admittedly failed to comply with the requirement of Section 1317.2(b) of the School Code that it develop a written policy regarding expulsions of a weapon. More important, the District failed to provide its superintendent with the discretion to modify discipline that is granted to the superintendent by Section 1317.2(c) of the School Code. . . .

Clearly, the legislature recognized that circumstances could arise that would require an exception to be made to the mandatory expulsion provision of Section 1317.2. Thus, the legislature expressly authorized the superintendent of each school district to recommend a modification of that requirement on a case-by-case basis. Implicit in that grant of authority is a grant of permission to the Board to consider an alternative to expulsion based upon the recommendation of the District's superintendent.

A school board may not make rules which are outside their grant of authority from the General Assembly. . . . We conclude that the Board exceeded its authority in adopting its "zero tolerance policy," which denies the superintendent, the Board and the students the exercise of discretion specifically provided by Section 1317.2 of the School Code and which frustrates the clear legislative intent that this statute not be blindly applied. . . .

Accordingly, the decision of the trial court is affirmed.

Board's Zero Tolerance Policy would surely be irrational if it subjects to punishment students who did not knowingly or consciously possess a weapon."[15]

The school board argued that the federal courts should defer to school officials and assume that their day-to-day decisions are rational. The appeals court rejected that argument, writing, "The fact that we must defer to the Board's rational decisions in school discipline cases does not mean that we must, or should, rationalize away its irrational decision."[16] The appeals court concluded that school officials could not shield themselves from liability for due process violations by "hiding behind a Zero Tolerance policy."[17]

A federal district court ruled that Mississippi school officials violated the rights of a sixth grader when they expelled him for

THE LETTER OF THE LAW

An Excerpt from Florida's Zero Tolerance Policy for Schools

It is the intent of the Legislature to promote a safe and supportive learning environment in schools, to protect students and staff from conduct that poses a serious threat to school safety, and to encourage schools to use alternatives to expulsion or referral to law enforcement agencies by addressing disruptive behavior through restitution, civil citation, teen court, neighborhood restorative justice, or similar programs. The Legislature finds that zero-tolerance policies are not intended to be rigorously applied to petty acts of misconduct and misdemeanors, including, but not limited to, minor fights or disturbances. The Legislature finds that zero-tolerance policies must apply equally to all students regardless of their economic status, race, or disability. . . .

Zero-tolerance policies may not require the reporting of petty acts of misconduct and misdemeanors to a law enforcement agency, including, but not limited to, disorderly conduct, disrupting a school function, simple assault or battery, affray, theft of less than $300, trespassing, and vandalism of less than $1,000.

Source: Florida Legislature, SB 1540. http://www.flsenate.gov/data/session/2009/Senate/bills/billtext/pdf/s1540.pdf.

carrying a Swiss Army knife to school. The school board expelled the student for one year pursuant to a zero-tolerance policy without considering the student's school record and previous conduct. The court wrote that it was "offended by the manner in which it [the school board] blindly meted out the student's punishment."[18]

More states should follow Florida and amend their zero tolerance policies. In June 2009, Florida amended its zero tolerance policy in public schools to require schools to distinguish between "petty acts of misconduct" and acts that pose a "serious threat to school safety."

Summary

Zero tolerance policies may be appropriate for serious weapons and drug offenses. Certainly, school officials should not tolerate any student behavior that threatens the safety of other students. True threats have no place in the school environment. And, of course, students should not knowingly bring weapons or illegal drugs to school. Zero tolerance policies, however, are being applied inflexibly, resulting in draconian punishments for relatively minor offenses. Zero tolerance policies too often result in zero judgment. School officials must use common sense and evaluate student discipline on a case-by-case basis. A student who brings a water pistol to school should not be subject to the same punishment as a student who brings a loaded gun.

A real danger exists that many zero tolerance policies are being applied in a racially discriminatory manner. African-American students are punished at a higher rate than other students. Studies have shown that socioeconomic and behavior issues do not explain away the disparities. Though more research is needed, there is a very real and obvious danger that the statistics are the result of biases—whether intentional or unintentional—in school.

There is also a very real possibility that zero tolerance policies violate the constitutional rights of students. Some punishments under zero tolerance policies violate the equal protection and due process clauses of the Fourteenth Amendment. When students of one race are punished more frequently than others are, there may be an equal protection violation. When students are punished automatically without any consideration of individual factors, there are due process problems. Students do not lose their constitutional rights simply by entering a public school. Too often, zero tolerance means zero judgment and an abdication of students' rights.

Safety Concerns Must Trump Fourth Amendment Rights in Public Schools

Public school officials must ensure that their students have a safe environment in which to learn. This is no easy task. Former Attorney General Janet Reno said, "Youth violence has been one of the greatest single crime problems we face in this country."[1] Violent school shootings have occurred across the nation, from Springfield, Oregon; to Paducah, Kentucky; to Pearl, Mississippi; to Santee, California. These horrors reverberate in the nation's collective conscience. The greatest tragedy, however, occurred in April 1999, in a shooting rampage by two disturbed youths at Columbine High School near Littleton, Colorado. The two young men, dressed in trench coats, opened fire, killing 12 students and one teacher.

Since the Columbine incident, many courts have recognized that school officials must be given a greater degree of flexibility to create a secure learning environment. School safety remains the paramount issue for school administrators as the United States fights its war against terrorism.[2] Drugs and violence are perennial problems among our nation's youth. One recent study found that more than 4 million students had participated in a serious fight at school.[3] A disturbing number of teenagers engages in drug use and brings weapons to school, despite the fact that the federal Gun-Free Schools Act requires states to pass laws that make schools expel for one year students who bring weapons to school.[4]

Students do not possess the same level of Fourth Amendment rights as adults.

Students do not lose all of their privacy rights when they enter the schoolhouse, but they do not possess the same level of constitutional rights as adults or minors in a nonschool setting, either. The need for school safety often trumps individual rights. Constitutional rights are, of course, important in the American democracy, but liberty must sometimes take a backseat to order. The primary purpose of public schools is to provide all children with a solid education. This cannot occur when violence, guns, and drugs disrupt the learning environment. The Fourth Amendment provides:

> The right of the people to be secure in their persons, houses, papers, and effects, against unreasonable searches and seizures, shall not be violated, and no Warrants shall issue, but upon probable cause, supported by Oath or affirmation, and particularly describing the place to be searched, and the persons or things to be seized.

This amendment is designed to safeguard a person's fundamental right to be let alone. It means that the police cannot come and rummage through someone's home unless they have probable cause to believe that he or she is harboring contraband

On April 20, 1999, students flee from Columbine High School near Little-ton, Colorado, under cover from police. Two teens on a suicide mission stormed the school, killing and wounding fellow students before turning the weapons on themselves. Twelve students and one teacher were killed, 21 other students were injured directly, and three people were injured while escaping.

there. Probable cause means that the police must have more than just a hunch to suspect that someone has illegal materials. They must be able to show evidence that suggests a likelihood of illegality. The police cannot search a home unless they have obtained a warrant signed by a neutral judge or magistrate. A warrant ensures that the judicial branch, often a magistrate, reviews the actions of other government officials. The require-ments of probable cause and a warrant are fundamental to tra-ditional Fourth Amendment jurisprudence. They are designed to curb governmental abuse of individual liberty.

These rights are impractical in the public school setting. School officials do not have the time to get a warrant from a judge every time they may need to search a student. To impose these requirements would make the orderly administration of the school a practical impossibility. As a result, the U.S. Supreme Court has made clear in a series of decisions that public school students do not possess the same level of rights as adults.

Students may be searched with less than probable cause.

In its landmark 1985 decision, *New Jersey v. T.L.O.*, the U.S. Supreme Court established a new Fourth Amendment standard for searches conducted by public school officials in the school setting. The case arose after school officials suspected two 14-year-old students of smoking in a school bathroom. One student admitted smoking, but the other student—known in court papers as T.L.O.—denied it.

An assistant principal then looked inside the second student's purse. He found a pack of cigarettes and also rolling papers, which he knew were associated with marijuana. At that point, he decided to conduct a full-scale search of the student's purse. He found a small amount of marijuana, a number of empty plastic bags, an index card with names of students who owed T.L.O. money, and two letters that implicated T.L.O. in drug dealing. The assistant principal turned the information

THE LETTER OF THE LAW

Gun-Free Schools Act, 20 U.S.C. 8921

[E]ach State receiving Federal funds under this Act shall have in effect a State law requiring local educational agencies to expel from school for a period of not less than one year a student who is determined to have brought a weapon to a school under the jurisdiction of local educational agencies in that State, except that such State law shall allow the chief administering officer of such local educational agency to modify such expulsion requirement for a student on a case-by-case basis.

over to the police. The student confessed to dealing drugs and the state brought delinquency charges against her.

The student argued that the search of her purse had violated her Fourth Amendment rights. The state countered that the Fourth Amendment does not apply to searches conducted by school officials. The New Jersey supreme court reasoned that students do retain their Fourth Amendment rights in school and concluded that the assistant principal had violated T.L.O.'s constitutional rights because he did not have reasonable suspicion to rummage through all the contents in the student's purse simply because he saw a pack of cigarettes.

The U.S. Supreme Court reversed the New Jersey supreme court's decision, determining that the school official's search was reasonable under the circumstances. The Court set up a so-called "reasonableness" standard for school searches:

> [T]he legality of a search of a student should depend simply on the reasonableness, under all the circumstances, of the search. Determining the reasonableness of any search involves a two-fold inquiry: first, one must consider whether the action was justified at its inception; second, one must determine whether the search as actually conducted was reasonably related in scope to the circumstances which justified the interference in the first place.[5]

According to the Court, this reasonableness standard "will spare teachers and school administrators the necessity of schooling themselves in the niceties of probable cause and permit them to regulate their conduct according to the dictates of reason and common sense."[6] Applying this standard to the facts of the case, the U.S. Supreme Court concluded that it was reasonable for the assistant principal to search the student's purse for cigarettes when a teacher had reported that the student had indeed smoked in the bathroom.

Random drug testing is essential for school safety and discipline.

Drug abuse among teenagers and even younger children remains a perennial problem. Children today are experimenting with drugs such as marijuana, ecstasy, and even cocaine at younger and younger ages. Many school districts have turned to drug testing in order to prevent further abuse.

FROM THE BENCH

New Jersey v. T.L.O., 469 U.S. 325 (1985)

By focusing attention on the question of reasonableness, the standard will spare teachers and school administrators the necessity of schooling and school administrators the necessity of schooling themselves in the niceties of probable cause and permit them to regulate their conduct according to the dictates of reason and common sense....

[T]he New Jersey Supreme Court also held that Mr. Choplick had no reasonable suspicion that the purse would contain cigarettes. This conclusion is puzzling. A teacher had reported that T.L.O. was smoking in the lavatory. Certainly this report gave Mr. Choplick reason to suspect that T.L.O. was carrying cigarettes with her; and if she did have cigarettes, her purse was the obvious place in which to find them. Mr. Choplick's suspicion that there were cigarettes in the purse was not an "inchoate and unparticularized suspicion or 'hunch,'" [*Terry v. Ohio*, 392 U.S.] at 27; rather, it was the sort of "common-sense [conclusion] about human behavior" upon which "practical people"—including government officials—are entitled to rely. [*United States v. Cortez*, 449 U.S. 411, 418 (1981)] Of course, even if the teacher's report were true, T.L.O. *might* not have had a pack of cigarettes with her; she might have borrowed a cigarette from someone else or have been sharing a cigarette with another student. But the requirement of reasonable suspicion is not a requirement of absolute certainty: "sufficient probability, not certainty, is the touchstone of reasonableness under the Fourth Amendment...." [*Hill v. California*, 401 U.S. 797, 804 (1971)] Because the hypothesis that T.L.O. was carrying cigarettes in her purse was itself not unreasonable, it is irrelevant that other hypotheses were also consistent with the teacher's accusation. Accordingly, it cannot be said that Mr. Choplick acted unreasonably when he examined T.L.O.'s purse to see if it contained cigarettes....

The U.S. Supreme Court has twice upheld school drug testing policies in *Vernonia School District v. Acton*[7] and *Board of Education of Independent School District No. 92 of Pottawatomie County v. Earls.*[8] In *Vernonia*, the Supreme Court ruled 6–3 in favor of an Oregon high school district policy of random drug testing for student athletes. In the *Earls* case, the Supreme Court ruled 5–4 in favor of an Oklahoma school

Our conclusion that Mr. Choplick's decision to open T.L.O.'s purse was reasonable brings us to the question of the further search for marihuana once the pack of cigarettes was located. The suspicion upon which the search for marihuana was founded was provided when Mr. Choplick observed a package of rolling papers in the purse as he removed the pack of cigarettes. Although T.L.O. does not dispute the reasonableness of Mr. Choplick's belief that the rolling papers indicated the presence of marihuana, she does contend that the scope of the search Mr. Choplick conducted exceeded permissible bounds when he seized and read certain letters that implicated T.L.O. in drug dealing. This argument, too, is unpersuasive. The discovery of the rolling papers concededly gave rise to a reasonable suspicion that T.L.O. was carrying marihuana as well as cigarettes in her purse. This suspicion justified further exploration of T.L.O.'s purse, which turned up more evidence of drug-related activities: a pipe, a number of plastic bags of the type commonly used to store marihuana, a small quantity of marihuana, and a fairly substantial amount of money. Under these circumstances, it was not unreasonable to extend the search to a separate zippered compartment of the purse; and when a search of that compartment revealed an index card containing a list of "people who owe me money" as well as two letters, the inference that T.L.O. was involved in marihuana trafficking was substantial enough to justify Mr. Choplick in examining the letters to determine whether they contained any further evidence. In short, we cannot conclude that the search for marihuana was unreasonable in any respect.

Because the search resulting in the discovery of the evidence of marihuana dealing by T.L.O. was reasonable, the New Jersey Supreme Court's decision to exclude that evidence from T.L.O.'s juvenile delinquency proceedings on Fourth Amendment grounds was erroneous. Accordingly, the judgment of the Supreme Court of New Jersey is *Reversed*.

district's policy of random drug testing for students involved in extracurricular activities.

Vernonia School District adopted its policy after a sharp increase in drug use among the student body in the late 1980s. School officials learned that student athletes were among the leaders of the school's drug culture. After holding a parent "input" night, they adopted a so-called "Athlete Drug Policy." James Acton, then a seventh grader, challenged the constitutionality of the policy on Fourth Amendment grounds. Acton, who wanted to play football, and his parents contended that the policy infringed on his privacy rights. They also argued that the Fourth Amendment generally required individualized suspicion. It did not provide for suspicion of an entire class of people based on their involvement in a particular activity. They pointed out that in the *New Jersey v. T.L.O.* case, the New Jersey school officials had suspicions that T.L.O was violating an anti-smoking rule. The drug testing policy in Vernonia, in contrast, tested students randomly, without regard to suspicion against any individual.

The U.S. Supreme Court majority ruled that the Constitution did not require public school officials to have individualized suspicion before drug testing student athletes. "Legitimate privacy expectations are even less with regard to student athletes," the Court wrote.[9] The Court reasoned that student athletes already submitted to preseason physical examinations and voluntarily subjected themselves to other forms of regulation. The majority also reasoned that the drug test results would not be given to the police or used to discipline students beyond suspension from the athletic team.

The Court also noted that drugs posed substantial risks to athletes: "Apart from psychological effects, which include impairment of judgment, slow reaction time, and a lessening of the perception of pain, the particular drugs screened by the District's Policy have been demonstrated to pose substantial physical risks to athletes."[10]

The Court concluded that three factors mandated a finding in favor of the school: first, decreased expectation of student privacy in the school setting; second, "the relative unobtrusiveness of the search;" and third, the severe need for the policy at the school.[11]

The U.S. Supreme Court revisited the issue of drug testing in public schools seven years later. As Vernonia had done, the Tecumseh, Oklahoma, school district adopted a random drug testing policy for all middle and high school students who wished to participate in any extracurricular activities. The school applied the policy to any extracurricular group sanctioned by the state secondary schools activities association. This meant that, in addition to sports teams, student groups such as the Academic Team, the Future Farmers of America, band, choir, and cheerleaders were tested.

Students Lindsay Earls, a member of the marching band, and Daniel James, who sought to become a member of the Academic Team, challenged the policy in federal court. They noted that the Vernonia policy upheld by the Supreme Court focused on the lessened privacy interests of student athletes, not all students involved in extracurricular activities.

Despite their arguments, a narrow majority of the U.S. Supreme Court sided with the school district. "A student's

FROM THE BENCH

Board of Education of Independent School District No. 92 of Pottawatomie County v. Earls, 536 U.S. 822 (2002)

Likewise, the need to prevent and deter the substantial harm of childhood drug use provides the necessary immediacy for a school testing policy. Indeed, it would make little sense to require a school district to wait for a substantial portion of its students to begin using drugs before it was allowed to institute a drug testing program designed to deter drug use.

privacy interest is limited in a public school environment where the State is responsible for maintaining discipline, health, and safety," the Court's opinion said. "Schoolchildren are routinely required to submit to physical examinations and vaccinations against disease."[12] The Court also made note of evidence that drug abuse among students was still a major problem that made drug testing a reasonable practice.

Schools should use advances in technology to ensure school safety.

Too many young people have access to firearms in our society. Students carrying guns to school has become a recipe for

FROM THE BENCH

Vernonia School District v. Acton, 515 U.S. 646 (1995)

As the text of the Fourth Amendment indicates, the ultimate measure of the constitutionality of a governmental search is "reasonableness." At least in a case such as this, where there was no clear practice, either approving or disapproving the type of search at issue, at the time the constitutional provision was enacted, whether a particular search meets the reasonableness standard "'is judged by balancing its intrusion on the individual's Fourth Amendment interests against its promotion of legitimate governmental interests.'" ... Where a search is undertaken by law enforcement officials to discover evidence of criminal wrongdoing, this Court has said that reasonableness generally requires the obtaining of a judicial warrant. ... Warrants cannot be issued, of course, without the showing of probable cause required by the Warrant Clause. But a warrant is not required to establish the reasonableness of *all* government searches; and when a warrant is not required (and the Warrant Clause therefore not applicable), probable cause is not invariably required either. A search unsupported by probable cause can be constitutional, we have said, "when special needs, beyond the normal need for law enforcement, make the warrant and probable-cause requirement impracticable." We have found such "special needs" to exist in the public school context.

disaster. Many schools have used metal detectors in order to prevent guns from being brought onto school grounds. The Supreme Court of Pennsylvania ruled in the 1999 case *In Re F.B.* that the use of metal scanners by police officers in a Philadelphia high school did not violate the Fourth Amendment rights of students.[13] Noting that metal detectors and X-ray machines are used regularly in airports, the court determined that the privacy interest was minimal. "The actual character of the intrusion suffered by the students during the search is no greater than that regularly experienced by millions of people as they pass through an airport," the court wrote.[14]

Schools are also permitted to install cameras that monitor different areas of the school. One author on the subject of school safety recommends that school officials "provide additional surveillance for restrooms, whether by adults or surveillance cameras" and "install video cameras throughout the school in any place where violence is likely to occur."[15]

Searches of school property are reasonable.

Students have little if any reasonable expectation of privacy while they are on school property. Students do place personal items in their desks and lockers. The school, however, owns those desks and lockers. Assuming school officials have provided written notice that these places are subject to search, students simply do

FROM THE BENCH

In Re Patrick Y., 746 A.2d 405 (Md. App. 2000)

School lockers . . . are not regarded as the personal property of the student. They are classified as school property, part of the "plant of the school" . . . , and no doubt because of that, school officials are permitted to search the lockers as they could any other school property. No probable cause is required; nor is any reasonable suspicion required.

not have reasonable Fourth Amendment claims. School officials retain a master, or pass, key that enables them to search lockers for contraband. Several courts have determined that students possess no reasonable expectation of privacy in their lockers.[16]

Summary

We live in a violent world. The recent spate of school shootings and the terrorist threat both at home and abroad make safety a serious issue for school administrators. School officials need flexibility in order to respond to such challenges. Students' constitutional rights to privacy under the Fourth Amendment are important, but they must take a backseat when school officials have reasonable concerns about school safety.

School officials must not be hampered by the requirements of probable cause. They do not have time to obtain a warrant every time they need to search a student or a student's possessions. The day-to-day realities of the school environment often require quick judgments based on common sense and experience. Unless the search or seizure is unusually egregious, it will likely be a judgment call for school administrators.

Students Must Not Lose Their Fourth Amendment Rights

School officials understandably wish to protect students from harm. In fact, the law requires that they provide a safe learning environment. The rush to protect children, however, must not lead to an evisceration of fundamental constitutional freedoms. Young people still possess a degree of privacy even in the school environment. The Supreme Court requires individualized suspicion even under *New Jersey v. T.L.O.*

Even though the U.S. Supreme Court upheld the search of the student's person in *New Jersey v. T.L.O.*, the Court recognized several important principles. First, the Court noted that the Fourth Amendment applies to searches conducted by public school officials. The school had argued during the litigation that the Fourth Amendment applied only to searches carried out by law enforcement officials. The state also argued that because school officials acted like parents—*in loco parentis*—they should be treated like parents and not be subject to the Constitution. If a parent unreasonably searches a child's room, the child cannot sue his or her parent under the Constitution. The school argued that a student should not be able to sue a school official for an unreasonable search. The Court rejected these arguments, explaining that school officials act as representatives of the state, which makes them, like all other governmental employees, subject to the dictates of the Constitution.

The Court also rejected the argument that students lose all privacy interests when they enter school grounds. Instead, the justices recognized that school officials could search a student when they had reasonable suspicion that the student was violating a school rule or carrying contraband. In other words, school officials have to put forth facts showing that they have individualized suspicion that a particular student should be searched.

The Court also articulated a new standard that school officials must follow. First, the search must be justified at the beginning. Second, the search must be "reasonably related in

FROM THE BENCH

New Jersey v. T.L.O., 469 U.S. 325 (1985)

If school authorities are state actors for purposes of the constitutional guarantees of freedom of expression and due process, it is difficult to understand why they should be deemed to be exercising parental rather than public authority when conducting searches of their students. More generally, the Court has recognized that "the concept of parental delegation" as a source of school authority is not entirely "consonant with compulsory education laws." Today's public school officials do not merely exercise authority voluntarily conferred on them by individual parents; rather, they act in furtherance of publicly mandated educational and disciplinary policies. . . . In carrying out searches and other disciplinary functions pursuant to such policies, school officials act as representatives of the State, not merely as surrogates for the parents, and they cannot claim the parents' immunity from the strictures of the Fourth Amendment.

scope to the circumstances" that made the search justifiable in the first place. This means that the search "must be reasonably related to the objectives of the search and not excessively intrusive in light of the age and sex of the student and the nature of the infraction."[1]

Not all the justices of the Supreme Court agreed that the search of the student's purse in *T.L.O.* was constitutional. Justice John Paul Stevens wrote in his dissenting opinion that "the rule the Court adopts today is so open-ended that it may make the Fourth Amendment virtually meaningless in the school context."[2]

The Supreme Court has gone too far in ruling on drug testing.

The U.S. Supreme Court has narrowly upheld random drug testing programs of student athletes in *Vernonia School Dist. v. Acton* (1995) and *Board of Education of Independent School District No. 92 of Pottawatomie County v. Earls* (2002). These decisions, however, were not made without controversy or without substantial dissent among the Court's members. Three justices of the Court dissented in *Vernonia* and four dissented in *Earls*.

Sandra Day O'Connor, regarded as a generally conservative justice during her quarter-century tenure on the Supreme Court, dissented in both cases. She argued that students should only be searched under the Fourth Amendment when school officials possessed individualized suspicion. She wrote, "For most of our constitutional history, mass, suspicionless searches have been generally considered per se unreasonable within the meaning of the Fourth Amendment."[3]

Justice O'Connor chastised her colleagues in the majority for failing to appreciate the necessity of individualized suspicion as a requirement of Fourth Amendment jurisprudence. She reasoned that just as the police may not drug test every person who leaves a neighborhood where drugs are common, school officials may not drug test any student simply for participating in an extracurricular activity.

O'Connor argued that school officials could install a drug testing program that enabled school officials to carry out drug tests based on reasonable suspicion. Acknowledging that mass testing without suspicion may be more effective in curtailing drug use, O'Connor wrote, "there is nothing new in the realization that Fourth Amendment protections come with a price."[4] To O'Connor and her fellow dissenting justices, the majority sacrificed students' Fourth Amendment freedoms on the altar of expediency.

Four members of the Supreme Court also disagreed with the Court's decision in *Board of Education v. Earls*, a case that upheld a random drug testing program for students involved in extracurricular activities. Justice Ruth Bader Ginsburg, a generally liberal justice, wrote a stinging dissent: "The particular testing program upheld today is not reasonable, it is capricious, even perverse; Petitioners' policy targets for testing a student population least likely to be at risk from illicit drugs and their damaging effects."[5] Ginsburg also cited evidence that high school students who participate in extracurricular activities are less likely than their more inactive peers to experiment with illegal drugs.

Even though the U.S. Supreme Court has ruled twice that random drug testing programs in high schools are constitutional,

QUOTABLE

Justice Sandra Day O'Connor, dissenting in *Vernonia School Dist. v. Acton*, 515 U.S. 646 (1995)

[I]ntrusive, blanket searches of schoolchildren, most of whom are innocent, for evidence of serious wrongdoing are not part of any traditional school function of which I am aware. Indeed, many schools, like many parents, prefer to trust their children unless given reason to do otherwise. As James Acton's father said on the witness stand, "[suspicionless testing] sends a message to children that are trying to be responsible citizens . . . that they have to prove that they're innocent . . . , and I think that kind of sets a bad tone for citizenship."

litigation will surely continue. Commentators predict that students will file more challenges under their respective state constitutions.[6] A state supreme court may even interpret a state constitution to provide greater individual freedom than the federal Constitution.

Strip searches are too invasive under the Fourth Amendment.

Among the most invasive type of searches are strip searches in which a person is forced to undress. This procedure can cause a great deal of embarrassment and humiliation to students forced to undergo it. School law expert Nathan Essex wrote in his book *School Law and the Public Schools: A Practical Guide for Educational Leaders* that "strip searches should be avoided except under extreme circumstances involving the health and safety of other students."[7]

Many courts have ruled that strip searches violate the Fourth Amendment. Most significantly, in June 2009, the U.S. Supreme Court ruled that California middle school officials violated the Fourth Amendment rights of a student when they subjected her to a strip search because they wrongfully suspected her of carrying prescription drugs. The Court ruled in *Safford Unified School District v. Redding* that school officials must have "reasonable suspicion of danger or of resort to underwear for hiding evidence of wrongdoing before a search can reasonably make the quantum leap from outer clothes and backpacks to exposure of intimate parts."[8]

School officials had heard that some students had prescription pills at school. One official had confiscated four pills of prescription-strength ibuprofen pills and a pill planner from a student. The student said the planner and the pills were the property of Savana Redding, another student.

School officials then searched Redding's purse and found nothing. The school officials then instructed a school nurse to conduct a degrading search during which Redding had to pull out the elastic of her underwear and expose her breast and pelvic areas. The majority of the U.S. Supreme Court deemed this search excessive, given that the pills were not dangerous and that there was no reason to suspect that Redding might be carrying the pills in her underwear. The Court concluded:

> In sum, what was missing from the suspected facts that pointed to Savana was any indication of danger to the students from the power of the drugs or their quantity,

FROM THE BENCH

Safford Unified School District #1 v. Redding, 129 S.Ct. (2009)

Savana's subjective expectation of privacy against such a search is inherent in her account of it as embarrassing, frightening, and humiliating. The reasonableness of her expectation (required by the Fourth Amendment standard) is indicated by the consistent experiences of other young people similarly searched, whose adolescent vulnerability intensifies the patent intrusiveness of the exposure. . . . The common reaction of these adolescents simply registers the obviously different meaning of a search exposing the body from the experience of nakedness or near undress in other school circumstances. Changing for gym is getting ready for play; exposing for a search is responding to an accusation reserved for suspected wrongdoers and fairly understood as so degrading that a number of communities have decided that strip searches in schools are never reasonable and have banned them no matter what the facts may be. . . .

The indignity of the search does not, of course, outlaw it, but it does implicate the rule of reasonableness as stated in *T.L.O.*, that "the search as actually conducted [be] reasonably related in scope to the circumstances which justified the interference in the first place." . . . The scope will be permissible, that is, when it is "not excessively intrusive in light of the age and sex of the student and the nature of the infraction." . . .

Here, the content of the suspicion failed to match the degree of intrusion. Wilson knew beforehand that the pills were prescription-strength ibuprofen and over-the-counter naproxen, common pain relievers equivalent to two Advil, or one Aleve. He must have been aware of the nature and limited threat of the and any reason to suppose that Savana was carrying pills in her underwear. We think that the combination of these deficiencies was fatal to finding the search reasonable.

Some lower courts, even before the U.S. Supreme Court's historic ruling in the Savana Redding case, had invalidated strip searches. For example, a federal district court ruled in *Bell v.*

---

specific drugs he was searching for, and while just about anything can be taken in quantities that will do real harm, Wilson had no reason to suspect that large amounts of the drugs were being passed around, or that individual students were receiving great numbers of pills.

Nor could Wilson have suspected that Savana was hiding common painkillers in her underwear. Petitioners suggest, as a truth universally acknowledged, that "students . . . hid[e] contraband in or under their clothing," Reply Brief for Petitioners 8, and cite a smattering of cases of students with contraband in their underwear, *id.*, at 8-9. But when the categorically extreme intrusiveness of a search down to the body of an adolescent requires some justification in suspected facts, general background possibilities fall short; a reasonable search that extensive calls for suspicion that it will pay off. But nondangerous school contraband does not raise the specter of stashes in intimate places, and there is no evidence in the record of any general practice among Safford Middle School students of hiding that sort of thing in underwear; neither Jordan nor Marissa suggested to Wilson that Savana was doing that, and the preceding search of Marissa that Wilson ordered yielded nothing. Wilson never even determined when Marissa had received the pills from Savana; if it had been a few days before, that would weigh heavily against any reasonable conclusion that Savana presently had the pills on her person, much less in her underwear.

In sum, what was missing from the suspected facts that pointed to Savana was any indication of danger to the students from the power of the drugs or their quantity, and any reason to suppose that Savana was carrying pills in her underwear. We think that the combination of these deficiencies was fatal to finding the search reasonable.

Marseilles Elementary School that a police officer called to an eighth-grade gym class violated the students' constitutional rights when he initiated a blanket search of more than 30 students in an attempt to locate missing money. According to the court, the officer violated the Fourth Amendment because he did not have any facts that gave him any individualized suspicion: "While it may be true there was reasonable suspicion to believe that someone in the gym class had stolen money, there were no facts that enabled Officer Long to particularize which students in the class might possess the money."[9]

The New Mexico Supreme Court upheld a jury verdict of more than $100,000 in favor of two high school students who were subjected to strip searches after a classmate reported her ring missing in class. The controversy arose after school officials detained the entire class for more than 30 minutes when the student reported the missing ring. Two students—one male and one female—were searched because they had raised their hands requesting permission to use the restroom. The female student had to lift her blouse in front of a school official, while the male student had to pull his underpants away from his waist and shake them. Neither student had the ring.

The students later sued school officials, claiming a violation of their Fourth Amendment rights. The state's supreme court focused on the fact that school officials did not have any reason to suspect these students of wrongdoing. The court concluded that the school officials' actions were "clearly excessive" and "extremely intrusive."[10] The court criticized school officials for violating the students' clearly established constitutional rights:

> The same common sense that compels the conclusion that a school official cannot strip a child naked without having some individualized basis to suspect that child of wrongdoing, also mandates that a child cannot be stripped to his boxer shorts by officials who have no reason to suspect him individually.[11]

School officials must also ensure that they do not conduct strip searches based on unreliable evidence. In *Fewless v. Board of Education of Wayland Union Schools*, a federal district court in Michigan ruled in favor of student Joseph Fewless, who was subjected to a fully nude search a day after an earlier, less invasive search turned up no evidence of drugs. School officials claimed they had authority to conduct both searches because several other students—who were facing discipline for destroying Fewless's property—told them that Fewless had hidden drugs in his private parts. The other students claimed Fewless told them he avoided detection by carefully hiding the drugs in his posterior.

According to the court, school officials should have known that the information provided by the other students was tainted by their desire to see Fewless punished: "The informants' credibility was of a highly questionable nature, given their potential ill motives."[12]

The court explained that there was no other corroborating evidence, such as the smell of marijuana, to indicate that Fewless possessed drugs. Additionally, school officials could have engaged in less intrusive conduct, such as searching the student's locker or calling the student's parents for additional information. The court concluded that school officials went too far in relying on the unsubstantiated allegations of other students, whom school officials should have surmised carried a grudge against Fewless.

Technological advances should not turn schools into prisons.

Technology often brings advances to society in unimaginably positive ways. For instance, the Internet affords students unparalleled educational opportunities. However, technology can also have a dark side if it is abused. For example, unfettered Internet use can lead to unneeded exposure to pornography and other harmful material. Similarly, schools must consider the privacy rights of students when they implement technology to upgrade safety.

School officials must not be overzealous in installing cameras that would unnecessarily compromise student privacy. Placing cameras in student locker rooms will certainly lead to lawsuits. A middle school in Tennessee faced a million-dollar lawsuit filed by the parents of 17 students who were angry over the placement of cameras in locker rooms. According to the suit, school officials provided no notice to the students that the locker rooms were under surveillance.[13] Furthermore, the lawsuit alleged that the images of their children were viewed over the Internet by the security company in charge of the cameras.

The larger danger posed by the influx of technological security measures is that it may foster a sense in schoolchildren that "Big Brother" is watching. Too much security might lead to a situation in which students feel more like prisoners than pupils. In *New Jersey v. T.L.O.*, the U.S. Supreme Court wrote: "We are not yet ready to hold that the schools and the prisons need be equated for purposes of the Fourth Amendment."[14]

Professors Crystal Garcia and Sheila Suess Kennedy write in a law journal article:

> As technology becomes more sophisticated, it is by no means clear what sorts of devices will be held to constitute a violation of a reasonable expectation of privacy and, thus, a search for purposes of Fourth Amendment analysis. Once a particular method is deemed to be a search . . . it must meet the criteria for reasonableness even in the constitutionally permissive corridors of our public schools.[15]

Students have a right to privacy in their personal possessions at school.

Students do retain a degree of privacy protection in their personal possessions at school. The U.S. Supreme Court reiterated this point in the *T.L.O.* decision: "In short, schoolchildren may find it necessary to carry with them a variety of legitimate, noncontraband items, and there is no reason to conclude that they have necessarily waived all rights to privacy in such items merely by bringing them onto school grounds."[16]

Some courts have given little consideration to students' Fourth Amendment rights when searches occur on school grounds and particularly within school property. Other courts, though, have recognized that students do retain a reasonable expectation of privacy in their lockers.[17] Professor Essex wrote, "Barring an emergency, indiscriminate searches of students' lockers are indefensible and illegal."[18]

Summary

Students do not possess the same level of constitutional rights as adults in nonschool settings, particularly in the area of the Fourth Amendment. School safety in the post-Columbine era has caused many school officials to institute increased measures to ensure safety. Whether these measures involve installing new technological advances, instituting the wearing of identification badges, or conducting more searches of lockers or even bodies, there is no doubt that students' Fourth Amendment rights are in a precarious position.

Students' constitutional rights must not be swallowed in the drive to create a safe environment. The classroom is the first place that students have the chance to learn about the Constitution and governmental power. If students learn that they have no privacy rights in school, what impressions will they take away about the importance of constitutional freedoms in our society?

School Dress Codes Are Constitutional

School officials face a daunting task in providing students with a safe learning environment. Violence in school has become a nightmarish reality. The peak of that violence occurred in April 1999, at Columbine High School near Littleton, Colorado. Unfortunately, Columbine was not an isolated incident. School shootings have occurred in many other places. At times, students have been victimized for their sneakers, sports jackets, and other sought-after items.

One way many school districts across the country have sought to make schools safer is by implementing dress codes and uniform requirements. A typical uniform policy requires students to wear certain clothes, such as blue shirts and white pants. A dress code policy generally states what type of clothes a student may *not* wear. Standard dress codes will usually forbid T-shirts with sexual slogans or advertisements for tobacco or alcohol

60

products, short shorts, torn jeans, sagging jeans, spandex, halter tops, and clothes that expose the midriff area.

Dress requirements are passed for many reasons other than safety. Some students may feel ostracized because they cannot afford the latest fashions that are popular among their classmates. Other students wear clothing of certain colors to identify with or to show support for a particular gang.

Proponents of dress codes and uniforms argue that they reduce violence, lessen peer pressure, create a more positive learning environment, promote unity of spirit, and do not violate the constitutional rights of students and their parents. Dress codes and uniforms allow school officials to distinguish students from nonstudents on school grounds, preventing trespassers who might cause harm at the school. Others believe that dress codes decrease student-to-student sexual harassment and help prepare students for being part of the workforce.[1]

Uniforms help make schools safer places and improve learning.

Requiring uniforms makes it easier for school officials to identify nonstudents on campus. Those who enter the school campus for bad purposes can be identified more quickly. Additionally, when all students dress in the same manner, it eliminates competition over clothing choices. Students spend more time concentrating on their schoolwork and less time focusing on what they and their classmates are wearing. Many school principals and other officials have noted the positive effect of uniforms. They have reported that uniforms have boosted the school's image in the community, have improved school discipline, decreased peer pressure, raised school spirit, and helped promote safety.[2] Even then-president Bill Clinton endorsed the idea of school uniforms in his 1996 State of the Union address. He said, "If it means that teenagers will stop killing each other over designer jackets, then our public schools should be able to require their students to

(continues on page 65)

An excerpt from the Dress Code for Julian Union High School

Julian Union High School District is a place of learning and business. Our school is not the place for "fashion statements". Student dress and appearance should reflect this philosophy. Students are expected to exercise good judgment regarding their attire and grooming so as not to disrupt the educational environment and to establish a healthy school climate. Clothing must be clean, in good repair, and worn in such a manner as to exercise good taste and not to detract from the learning environment. Students' attire should be neat, clean, and appropriate for the school setting.

The following are NOT permitted:

1. Bare feet while at school or school-sponsored activities. Skate shoes, slippers or steel-toed shoes. For safety reasons teachers will require appropriate footwear. Appropriate footwear would be: tennis shoes, and dress shoes, and sandals.

2. Exposed midriffs: Tops must be long enough to be tucked in. Halters, backless, strapless, tube top, or spaghetti strap shirts; low cut blouses; any cleavage or see-through clothing. Appropriate tops would only allow the neck, head, and arms below the shoulder to be shown.

3. Clothing cut in such a way as to display bare skin or underwear. All straps or suspenders will be fastened.

4. Spiked belts, collars, cuffs, chains, or wallet chains of any length.

5. Hats/caps worn in the classroom, hallways, or other buildings except as required for health or safety purposes. Headgear, including hat, caps, nets, bandanas, etc., cannot be worn in any building except as required for health or safety purposes.

6. Slogans or logos, which contain profanity, obscenity, or that advertise or depict cigarettes or tobacco products, alcohol, drugs, or sexual acts. No pride slogans or logos, or language demeaning to any person or group, or anything that is considered by the administration to be in poor taste or demeaning to any person or group, will be displayed on shirts, blouses or articles of clothing.

7. Pajamas, sleepwear or slippers. (Except when part of approved "spirit day").

8. Sagging pants or underwear showing. Pants will be worn at waist.

9. Men's sleeveless undershirts.

10. Any clothing considered gang attire, as determined by administration.

11. The school administration may disallow other types of clothing that may jeopardize a safe and orderly environment for the students and school staff.

So as to clarify the dress code and make sure expectations are well understood, this next section is provided to take away any misunderstanding.

- No cleavage may show.

- No bare skin showing the body's midriff may be seen at any time. Therefore, no see-through tops or coverlets which cover a top that would violate this rule.

- No visible underwear of any kind.

- Shorts, skirts, and dresses must reach below the end of the fingers when student's arms are extended at the student's side.

For each infraction of the dress code, the following procedure should be followed:

- Student receives a Dress Code Violation Slip from a teacher and comes directly to the office.

- The student is given "lo[a]ner clothing" for the remainder of the day. The clothing which caused the infraction will be confiscated and kept until the next day.

- Students will return the "lo[a]ner clothing" the next day or the student will be billed $10 for the clothing.

The following consequences will result for each subsequent violation:

1. On the First offense student receives a warning;

2. On the Second offense student receives an after-school detention.

3. On the Third offense student receives a Saturday school.

4. Any subsequent offense will result in suspension.

Source: Dress Code for Julian Union High School. http://julian.ca.schoolwebpages.com/education/components/docmgr/default.php?sectiondetailid=1025.

In his 1996 State of the Union, President Bill Clinton supported tough anticrime measures to protect students and advocated the use of school uniforms as a way to deter violence. Seated behind the president is Vice President Al Gore.

(continued from page 61)
wear school uniforms."[3] Clinton also stated: "If it means that the schoolrooms will be more orderly, more disciplined, and that our young people will learn to evaluate themselves by what they are on the inside instead of what they're wearing on the outside, then our public schools should be able to require their students to wear school uniforms."[4]

Clinton cited the impressive results of a mandatory school uniform policy adopted in Long Beach, California. School officials from Long Beach claimed that the policy had led to a marked decrease in student disciplinary problems. Statistics from the Long Beach Unified School District show a significant decline in school crime. For example, in the school's "Grades K–8 School Crime Report Summary," the number of reported sex offenses dropped from 57 to 15 during the first year of uniforms. Similarly, the number of assault and battery crimes dropped from 319 to 214.

Following the president's 1996 State of the Union address, the Department of Education distributed a *Manual on School Uniforms* to more than 16,000 school districts nationwide. The handbook provided that, "In response to growing levels of violence in our schools, many parents, teachers, and school officials have come to see school uniforms as one positive and creative way to reduce discipline problems and increase school safety."[5]

Some commentators stress that dress codes and uniforms can directly reduce violence. They argue that schools should ban types of clothing, such as trench coats and baggy pants, which enable students to hide weapons easily. Carol Silverman Saunders, author of the book *Safe At School*, wrote, "If Columbine High School had outlawed the wearing of trench coats, the shooters would not have been able to hide their guns."[6]

A dress code or uniform policy will also prevent students from wearing gang-related apparel, which was the main reason that many schools adopted dress codes in the first place. Students affiliated with gangs wear certain kinds of clothing and special colors to denote their affinity for a particular gang.

For this reason, some state laws empower school officials to ban gang-related apparel.

Uniforms and dress codes also serve as an equalizer for kids from families with fewer financial resources. Studies have shown that uniforms can reduce fashion wars and are "social equalizers" that promote acceptance of others.[7] If students are less distracted about clothing, they can also concentrate more on their studies.

Uniforms do not violate the constitutional rights of students.

The First Amendment protects more than just verbal speech. There are also certain forms of expressive conduct—such as the

QUOTABLE

President Bill Clinton, State of the Union Address, January 23, 1996

Our . . . challenge is to provide Americans with the educational opportunities we will all need for this new century. In our schools, every classroom in America must be connected to the information superhighway, with computers and good software, and well-trained teachers. . . .

Every diploma ought to mean something. I challenge every community, every school and every state to adopt national standards of excellence; to measure whether schools are meeting those standards; to cut bureaucratic red tape so that schools and teachers have more flexibility for grass-roots reform; and to hold them accountable for results. . . .

I challenge every state to give all parents the right to choose which public school their children will attend; and to let teachers form new schools with a charter they can keep only if they do a good job. . . .

I challenge our parents to become their children's first teachers. Turn off the TV. See that the homework is done. And visit your children's classroom. No program, no teacher, no one else can do that for you.

Source: President Bill Clinton, State of the Union Address, January 23, 1996. http://odur.let. rug.nl/~usa/P/bc42/speeches/sud96wjc.htm.

wearing of black armbands—that deserve free speech protection. In *Spence v. Washington*, the U.S. Supreme Court established a two-part test for determining whether expressive conduct merits First Amendment protection. First, the expressive conduct had to convey a particularized message. Second, the message had to be one that many people would likely understand.[8]

Proponents of dress code and uniform policies argue that a great deal of student clothing does not qualify as expressive conduct because it doesn't contain a particularized message. They also argue that dress code policies are passed for many legitimate reasons that are unrelated to stifling freedom of expression.

Although the U.S. Supreme Court has not yet examined a student dress code case, it did provide a glimpse of how it might rule if such a case came up. In the landmark 1969 student free speech case, *Tinker v. Des Moines Independent Community School District*, the U.S. Supreme Court ruled that school officials violated the free expression rights of several students when they suspended the students for wearing black armbands to school. The Court ruled that school officials must reasonably forecast that a particular form of student expression will cause a substantial disruption of school activities or invade the rights of others before they can censor that expression. Unlike the black armbands in the *Tinker* case, some student clothing, such as gang-related apparel or racially insensitive clothing, may create a substantial disruption. For instance, if students wear "White Power" T-shirts, a school official could reasonably forecast that the T-shirts will exacerbate racial tensions at the school.

The *Tinker* case, however, may not even apply to most student clothing cases. In its ruling, the Supreme Court distinguished the typical clothing controversy from the wearing of black armbands as a form of political protest. The Court wrote:

> The problem posed by the present case does not relate to regulation of the length of skirts or the type of clothing, to hairstyle, or deportment. It does not concern aggressive, disruptive action or even group demonstrations.

Our problem involves direct, primary First Amendment rights akin to "pure speech."[9]

This passage indicates that the Court would not be nearly as concerned with a dispute over clothing as with pure political speech. Furthermore, the U.S. Supreme Court *has* curtailed the free expression rights of public school students since the 1969 *Tinker* decision. In two decisions in the 1980s—*Bethel School District v. Fraser*[10] and *Hazelwood School District v. Kuhlmeier*[11]—a more conservative Supreme Court than the one that decided *Tinker* sided with school officials in student First Amendment cases. Then, in a 2007 decision—*Morse v. Frederick*[12]—the Court also sided with school officials in a student speech case.

In *Bethel v. Fraser*, the Supreme Court ruled that school officials did not violate the First Amendment when they suspended a student for making a vulgar address before the student assembly. Though the case concerned verbal speech, the Court's reasoning also applies to dress code controversies. The Court wrote: "The undoubted freedom to advocate unpopular and controversial views in schools and classrooms must be balanced against the society's countervailing interest in teaching

THE LETTER OF THE LAW

Tennessee Code Annotated Section 49-6-4215

The local and county boards of education of this state are hereby authorized to promulgate and adopt rules and regulations to prohibit students in grades six through twelve (6–12) from wearing, while on school property, any type of clothing, apparel or accessory, including that which denotes such students' membership in or affiliation with any gang associated with criminal activities. The local law enforcement agency shall advise the local board, upon request, of gangs which are associated with criminal activity.

students the boundaries of socially appropriate behavior."[13] The Court also noted that school officials had the power to prohibit students from engaging in vulgar and lewd expression and conduct. This decision enables school officials to prevent any clothing that can be considered vulgar, lewd, or even plainly offensive. One federal court cited the *Fraser* case in upholding the suspension of a student for wearing a "Drugs Suck" T-shirt. Even though the shirt bore an antidrug message, the Court reasoned that the word *suck* had a vulgar connotation and could be banned under the *Fraser* precedent.[14]

In *Morse v. Frederick*, the Supreme Court ruled that school officials can prohibit student speech that the officials reasonably believe advocates illegal drug use.[15] This means that school officials can prohibit any student T-shirts advocating alcohol, drugs, or tobacco use.

Some lower courts will apply the *Tinker* standard to student dress cases. Others will first apply the two-part *Spence* test mentioned earlier. For example, a federal court in New Mexico rejected the First Amendment argument of a teenager who was suspended from school for wearing sagging pants in violation of the school's dress code. The teen argued that the sagging pants conveyed his message of support for African-American hip-hop culture. The court rejected this argument, finding that the wearing of sagging pants was not a form of protected expression.[16]

Most courts in recent years that have examined challenges to uniform and dress code policies have ruled them constitutional. For example, a federal appeals court upheld a Texas school district's uniform policy in *Littlefield v. Forney Independent School District*.[17]

School officials in this case adopted the policy for several reasons, including improving student performance, boosting student self-confidence, increasing attendance, and decreasing discipline problems. School officials also thought that the policy would lessen socioeconomic tensions between students who had money to purchase expensive clothes and those who did not. The appeals court determined that these were valid reasons for establishing the policy. The court rejected the argument that the policy was designed to suppress students' free expression rights under the First Amendment. "The record demonstrates that the Uniform Policy was adopted for other legitimate reasons unrelated to the suppression of student expression," the court wrote.[18]

Similarly, the court dismissed the argument that the mandatory uniform policy violated the students' parents' Fourteenth Amendment right to control the upbringing of their children. The court explained:

> While Parents may have a fundamental right in the upbringing and education of their children, this right does not cover the Parents' objection to a public school Uniform Policy. It has long been recognized that parental rights are not absolute in the public school context and can be subject to reasonable regulation.[19]

Another federal appeals court panel from the Fifth Circuit upheld a Louisiana school district's adoption of a uniform policy. A group of parents sued the school district, claiming that

FROM THE BENCH

Canady v. Bossier Parish School Board, 240 F.3d 437 (5th Cir. 2001)

The School Board's purpose for enacting the uniform policy is to increase test scores and reduce disciplinary problems throughout the school system. This purpose is in no way related to the suppression of student speech. Although students are restricted from wearing clothing of their choice at school, students remain free to wear what they want after school hours. Students may still express their views through other mediums during the school day.

the policy violated their children's First Amendment rights. The school board countered that since the adoption of the uniform policy, student test scores had increased and discipline problems dramatically declined.[20]

The legal test applied by the Fifth Circuit court in both the *Littlefield* and *Canady* cases was: (1) whether the school board had the power to enact the policy; (2) whether the school board's uniform policy furthered an important or substantial governmental interest; (3) whether the school board policy was unrelated to the suppression of free expression; and (4) whether the policy's incidental effects on free expression were no greater than necessary to facilitate the school board's interests.[21]

Another federal appeals court, the Ninth Circuit, has rejected a similar challenge to a dress code that prohibited all messages on clothing. The Ninth Circuit in *Jacobs v. Clark County School District* determined that the school uniform policy served several significant school interests, including: "(1) increasing student achievement; (2) promoting safety; and (3) enhancing a positive school environment."[22]

Schools boards certainly have the power to regulate student dress. Most states have laws that specifically give local school boards such power. School uniforms also further an interest of the highest order: protecting student safety and improving the learning environment. Restrictions on student dress are not designed to suppress free expression; rather, they are a way to improve the educational environment. Finally, some students may feel that their free expression rights have been violated. That incidental restriction, however, is minor when compared to the many positive benefits to be gained from a student dress code.

Summary

While some students and parents object to dress codes, the majority of school administrators recognize that well-drafted student dress codes help provide a better learning environment. Students need to learn how to dress for success. If a person goes on a job interview, he or she is expected to dress in appropriate attire. School should be no different. School should be more about discipline than fashion. School uniforms help decrease tensions in school, reduce socioeconomic differences, improve safety, and remove distractions. The vast majority of courts have upheld student dress policies against constitutional challenges. For all these reasons, students and parents should find nothing objectionable about school uniforms.

School Dress Codes Are Unconstitutional

Students do not lose their constitutional rights when they enter the schoolhouse door. Neither should they lose their individuality. Mandatory uniform and dress code policies restrict creativity and foster resentment in students. Such policies are a Band-Aid solution that does not solve the underlying problems facing society. They are politically popular policies with little, if any, proven effectiveness.

The American Civil Liberties Union (ACLU) conducted a series of discussions with students. It asked the students to propose ways to deal with the real problem of school violence. The students' suggestions were:

(1) Since school violence mirrors that of society at large, schools should seriously confront and discuss issues of racism and cultural conflict;

(2) "Safe corridor" programs should be supported to

73

protect the safety of students as they go to and from school;

(3) School entrances should be secured;

(4) More extracurricular activities and clubs should be established;

(5) Open-mike assemblies should be held on a regular basis to give students the opportunity to express themselves;

(6) Programs to help students find part-time jobs should be established; and

(7) Conflict resolution techniques should be taught.[1]

These suggestions from students themselves show that school officials would be better advised to address the underlying problems of violence and conflict than to restrict student dress. Restricting student dress may further alienate youths who already feel disconnected. If school officials want to help students, they should listen to them.

Uniform and dress code policies do not create greater security.

Uniforms and dress code policies do not really make schools any safer. Rather, they are, as Wendell Anderson wrote, "shallow solutions to deeper problems."[2] Security concerns are better addressed by talking to the students, not turning them into clones or robots. It is highly questionable whether uniforms actually lead to safer schools. One legal commentator wrote:

> If a student, gang member or not, wants to bring a weapon to school, a uniform is not going to prevent the student from doing so.... In order for schools to eliminate gang violence on campus, they should focus on the core of the problem—students' association with gangs—not the resulting violence or the mere meaning of certain clothing.[3]

One study found that uniforms do *not* lead to better discipline in schools. The study concluded that "student uniforms have no direct effect on substance use, behavioral problems, or attendance." The researchers added that "a negative effect of uniforms on student academic achievement was found."[4]

Furthermore, there may be a danger that certain dress code policies will be applied more harshly to minority students. One legal commentator wrote, "Dress codes may contain an inherent racial bias because they tend to focus on clothing associated with African-American gangs while ignoring other groups such as white supremacist gangs."[5]

Mandatory and restrictive uniform policies violate students' First Amendment rights.

The First Amendment protects far more than verbal expression. Freedom of speech and expression has wide meaning. The amendment also protects other forms of expressive conduct, such as the wearing of clothing. In 1969, the U.S. Supreme Court ruled in *Tinker v. Des Moines Independent Community School District* that public school officials violated the First Amendment when they suspended several students for wearing black armbands to protest U.S. involvement in the Vietnam War.

The Court wrote, "It can hardly be argued that either students or teachers shed their constitutional rights to freedom of speech or expression at the schoolhouse gate." The Court established the rule that school officials could not censor student expression unless they could reasonably forecast that the student expression would cause a substantial disruption or material interference with school activities or invade the rights of others. According to the Supreme Court, school officials may not restrict student expression based on "undifferentiated fear or apprehension." They must have a factual basis to reasonably forecast that a particular form of student expression will create disruption at school.

For example, many schools have decided to ban Confederate flag clothing. The officials believe that the Confederate flag is a racially divisive symbol that may inflame racial tensions. The school officials, however, must have some factual basis to make this decision. If school administrators can show that there is a history of racial tension at the school, they will likely prevail. Several courts have sided with school officials when they have pointed to actual racial tension or past disruptions involving the Confederate flag.[6]

On the other hand, at least one federal court has determined that school officials may not selectively ban Confederate flag clothing without some evidence of actual disruption at school. The Sixth U.S. Circuit Court of Appeals ruled that school officials violated the First Amendment rights of two students who wore Hank Williams Jr. concert T-shirts that carried an image of the Confederate flag. The court sided with the students for a number of reasons. First, the court was concerned that school officials were selectively discriminating against the Confederate flag, while allowing students to wear clothing depicting other possibly racially inflammatory symbols, such as portraits of radical civil rights leader Malcolm X. The court said, "The school's refusal to bar the wearing of this apparel along with the Confederate flag gives the appearance of a targeted ban, something that the Supreme Court has routinely struck down as a violation of the First Amendment."[7] Second, the school officials in this case could point to no disturbances caused by the Hank Williams Jr. T-shirts. The students had worn the shirts to school on many occasions without incident. The court of appeals therefore determined that the school officials failed to meet the *Tinker* substantial disruption standard.

Students wear many types of clothing to express a variety of messages or beliefs. Some students wear T-shirts with political slogans. Others wear clothes in support of their favorite athletic team. Others may wear clothing that signifies their religious or ethnic heritage. A person's dress is an important source of self-identity and self-expression.

Much of this expression does not cause disruptions or disturbances. It merely reflects young people's attempt to figure out who they are in the world. School officials should not be able to censor student expression under a dress code policy unless they can demonstrate that the student expression will cause a substantial disruption of school activities. Some lower courts have applied the *Tinker* standard to forbid school officials from punishing students for the wearing of certain clothing.

One federal court ruled that school officials could not prevent students from wearing sports-related clothing. The school had argued that a ban on sports team clothing would curtail gang influence in schools. School officials, however, failed to show any incidence of gang activity in the school district's elementary and middle schools. The court concluded that, without such evidence of gang activity or disruption, school officials failed to carry their burden.[8]

Another court in California ruled that school officials went too far in punishing a student for wearing Winnie-the-Pooh-themed socks. School officials had attempted to justify the broad dress code as a legitimate means to combat gang-related apparel and activity. The judge rejected that argument, writing that the policy was "not narrowly tailored to meet the school district's legitimate gang prevention interests."[9] The school district later backed down and lightened up on the enforcement

FROM THE BENCH

Jeglin v. San Jacinto Unified School District, 827 F. Supp. 1459 (C.D. Cal. 1993)

To impose discipline resulting from a public school student's use of free speech under the First Amendment school officials have the burden to show justification for their actions. In the absence of such justification they may not discipline a student for exercising those rights.

of the policy. They also agreed to pay $95,000 in attorney fees and court costs.[10]

In a similar case, a federal appeals court reinstated the First Amendment claims of a student who was suspended for allegedly violating a school dress code. The young man wore a Chicago White Sox jersey to school, which officials claimed was being used as attire by a certain gang. The court said that school officials had to provide a factual basis about specific gang activity at its school before it could punish the student for wearing the jersey.[11]

In another case, a federal district court judge ruled that school officials violated the First Amendment when they punished students for wearing T-shirts bearing the message: "The best of the night's adventures are reserved for people with nothing planned." School officials argued that such T-shirts violated a provision in the dress code prohibiting clothing that promotes alcohol. They also argued that the wearing of such shirts was disruptive to the educational environment. The judge concluded that the defendants had offered "no credible or competent evidence" that the shirts advertised liquor or caused any disruptions of the school environment. Instead, the judge relied on evidence submitted by the students that they wore the T-shirts to school many times without disruption or incident.[12]

School uniform policies must contain an opt-out provision for students with religious objections. One federal court refused to dismiss a First Amendment lawsuit filed by a student and his great-grandmother. The great-grandmother and the student believed that the school's uniform policy violated their religious beliefs. The great-grandmother thought that the wearing of uniforms demonstrates an allegiance to the Antichrist, "a being that requires uniformity, sameness, enforced conformity, and the absence of diversity."[13]

Catherine Hicks, the great-grandmother and guardian of student Aaron Ganues, sued the board of education, claiming that the board had violated her and Ganues's First Amendment right to free speech and their First Amendment right to freely exercise their religious faith. They argued that the school board's actions were subject to heightened judicial scrutiny because the board violated two fundamental rights—the right of free speech

Student Prevails in North Carolina School Uniform Dispute

January 11, 2000

The American Civil Liberties Union issued the following statement at the conclusion of Aaron Ganues and Catherine Hicks's school uniform case:

RALEIGH, NC—In a victory for religious freedom and students' rights, a nine-year-old public school student will no longer face suspension for not wearing a school uniform because doing so conflicted with his family's religious beliefs, the American Civil Liberties Union of North Carolina said today.

In a settlement with officials at McIver Elementary School in Halifax, Aaron Ganues, who was twice suspended for failure to wear the school uniform, will be allowed a religious exemption from wearing the uniform for the remainder of his public school education.

"I am so happy to go back to school," said Aaron, an honor student with a near-perfect attendance record.

The settlement was reached on the eve of a trial to decide the matter, in a case brought by the ACLU on behalf of Aaron and his guardian, Catherine Hicks. Last December, a federal court refused school official's request to dismiss the case and ordered a trial to begin on January 10.

In its order, the court held that Aaron and his guardian "have now raised a genuine issue of material fact as to the nature of the burden imposed upon their free exercise of religion by the school uniform policy." The Court also ordered mediation. Halifax County will also amend its school uniform policy to allow religious exemptions and will pay for the cost of Aaron's schooling while he was out of the Halifax school system.

"This is a bright day for Aaron and for the First Amendment's promise of religious freedom," said Deborah Ross, Executive and Legal Director of the ACLU of North Carolina. "No child should be denied a public school education for failing to comply with a school uniform policy that conflicts with his family's religious beliefs."

Source: http://www.aclu.org/news/NewsPrint.cfm?ID=7785&c=156.

and the right to the free exercise of religion. The federal court agreed and would not dismiss the lawsuit.

School officials eventually settled the case with the plaintiffs after the judge refused to dismiss the case. Under the settlement, Ganues did not have to wear the school uniform and the school board agreed to amend its uniform policy by including a way out for those with religious objections to the policy. Deborah Ross, executive director for the American Civil Liberties Union of North Carolina, said, "No child should be denied a public school education for failing to comply with a school uniform policy that conflicts with his family's religious beliefs."[14]

Students retain the right to wear protest logos.

Some courts have upheld school uniform policies. Courts, however, also recognize that students retain the right to demonstrate against dress code policies by wearing protest logos or armbands. Even the Department of Education's *Manual on School Uniforms* says that students retain the right to protest.

For example, federal courts upheld the constitutionality of Louisiana's Bossier Parish School Board's mandatory uniform

An Excerpt from the *Manual on School Uniforms*

A uniform policy may not prohibit students from wearing or displaying expressive items—for example, a button that supports a political candidate—so long as such items do not independently contribute to disruption by substantially interfering with discipline or with the rights of others. Thus, for example, a uniform policy may prohibit students from wearing a button bearing a gang insignia. A uniform policy may also prohibit items that undermine the integrity of the uniform, notwithstanding their expressive nature, such as a sweatshirt that bears a political message but also covers or replaces the type of shirt required by the uniform policy.

Source: http://www.ed.gov/updates/uniforms.html.

policy. In the same case, however, a federal district court judge ruled that school officials could not prohibit a student from wearing black armbands to protest the dress code.[15]

Enforced dress codes violate parents' rights to control the upbringing of their children.

Critics of restrictive dress code and mandatory school uniform policies also argue that they not only violate the constitutional rights of the students but also the constitutional rights of their parents. The Fourteenth Amendment prohibits states from depriving individuals "of life, liberty or property, without due process of law." One of the liberty interests is the fundamental right of parents to control the way their children are raised.

In its 1925 decision in *Pierce v. Society of Sisters*, the U.S. Supreme Court struck down an Oregon law that required all children to attend public schools. Several parents challenged the law, contending that they had the right to send their children to private schools instead. The U.S. Supreme Court agreed with the parents, writing that the Fourteenth Amendment's liberty interest included the right of parents "to direct the upbringing and education of children under their control."[16]

Some parents contend that school uniform policies infringe on their parental liberty interests in raising their children. Some parents have banded together to form groups dedicated to raising opposition to mandatory school dress regulations.[17] Tim Tillman, a father of three students in Florida, formed the Parental Action Committee to oppose a dress regulation in Polk County. He said, "This mandatory school uniform policy is un-American and is fundamentally wrong. The children in this community are being denied their freedom of political and religious expression."[18]

Summary

School law expert Nathan Essex warned that school officials must not swallow student free expression rights in their rush to create a safer environment. "Policies that do not recognize these rights are risky at best and may result in mounting legal challenges and unnecessary legal costs to school districts," he wrote. "School officials should be assured, within limits, that the First Amendment rights of students are protected as they strive to create and maintain safe schools."[19]

The movement to change school dress is not a solution to underlying problems in a society. It may provide a false sense of security. But, even worse, it stifles creativity and teaches students that they do not possess individual rights of self-expression.

The Future of Student Rights

S tudents possess more rights in theory than in practice. Since the massacre at Columbine, school officials have clamped down on any student expression deemed unusual or strange. They have instituted more security measures that leave student privacy in doubt.

There are several reasons for the decline of student rights. First, the U.S. Supreme Court is more conservative than it was in the time of *Tinker*. The *Tinker* court was headed by Chief Justice Earl Warren. As Nadine Strossen explains: "The Court that issued the *Tinker* ruling, under the leadership of Chief Justice Earl Warren, was the most protective of constitutional rights that we have ever seen."[1] The Supreme Court, over the past few decades, under the leadership of Warren Burger, William Rehnquist, and the current chief justice, John G. Roberts Jr., has not been as vigilant in protecting the constitutional rights of students and other marginalized groups.

The Burger and Rehnquist courts decided the *Fraser* and *Hazelwood* cases. Both of these decisions curtailed the rights of students and limited the impact of the *Tinker* case. Matthew Fraser, the student litigant in the *Bethel v. Fraser* case, goes so far as to say that the case bearing his name overruled the *Tinker* decision.[2]

Second, students unfortunately now live in the age of Columbine. It is hard to describe the incredible effect that the Columbine shooting has had on the nation's schools. Arguably, only the terrorist attacks of September 11, 2001, has had a more devastating impact on the nation's collective conscience in the present generation. As David L. Hudson Jr. wrote, "The post-Columbine period has seen a surge in the implementation of dress-code and zero-tolerance policies and a crackdown on student Internet speech."[3]

Finally, the fear of new technology—the Internet—has made school officials less tolerant of student rights. In several instances, school officials have punished students for material they created on the Internet even when the students did not create the material on school computers. This reaction is predictable. Throughout history, government has responded to the development of new technologies with a period of overregulation and control. For example, after Johannes Gutenberg developed the first printing press between 1439 and 1450, religious leaders established the first censorship board and issued the first list of banned books. In 1915, the Supreme Court denied First Amendment protection to film, in part because the justices feared it would be a particularly effective way of corrupting youth. It was not until 1952 that the Court extended First Amendment protection to film.[4]

Many school officials have clamped down on students who criticize or lampoon school officials online. Sometimes the actions of school officials seem overblown, but at other times school officials appeared quite justified. Students have defamed teachers,

A former Republican governor of California, Chief Justice Earl Warren led the Supreme Court in its decision to outlaw racial segregation in public schools and later headed the commission investigating the assassination of President John F. Kennedy. His court also strongly supported the rights of students.

assumed their identities online, and made threats. The First Amendment does not protect speech that is defamatory, fraudulent, or truly threatening. These actions usually are not protected by the First Amendment.[5] Most courts have held that student online speech—even student speech created off-campus—can be prohibited if it creates a substantial disruption at school.

A related problem is cyberbullying, in which students have bullied and harassed other students online. Online expert Nancy Willard has written: "School personnel and policymakers have recognized that the consequences of bullying can be significant. Both bullies and victims are at high risk of suffering from serious health, safety, and educational risks."[6] She explains that before school officials punish students for off-campus, online speech there should be a nexus between the online speech and the school community that has a real and disruptive impact.[7]

Even the United States Congress had entered the fray over cyberbullying after the tragic suicide of a 13-year-old girl in Missouri, Megan Meier, who was subjected to taunts and harassment on the Internet.[8]

In this day and age, school officials must show respect for student rights. Only by speaking to students and providing them an outlet can school officials understand their problems, fears, and feelings of alienation. Commentator Stuart Leviton explains that school administrators need to show more respect for student rights:

> While parents and schools must inculcate youth with certain values, school administrators should include students in the selection of the values to be instilled. The silencing movement has not silenced students, and other puritanical and totalitarian methods have not stopped students from acting on their desires. Only by embracing a student-inclusive view and creating an environment where both students and school administrators mutually respect each other, listen to each other,

Tina Meier, of St. Charles, Missouri, holds two pictures of her teenage daughter, Megan, who committed suicide after receiving cruel messages on the online social network MySpace. On May 15, 2008, a federal grand jury in Los Angeles, California, indicted Lori Drew of St. Louis, Missouri, for her alleged role in perpetrating a hoax on MySpace against Megan Meier.

and try to incorporate ideas espoused by each other, can we hope to move toward a society that equally values students' rights and educators' goals.[9]

Summary

School officials should have a paramount concern for school safety. But the fundamental purpose of school is to educate young people. In a student Internet speech case, federal judge

Congressional Findings in H.R. 1966, the Megan Meier Cyberbullying Prevention Act

Congress finds the following:

(1) Four out of five of United States children aged 2 to 17 live in a home where either they or their parents have access to the Internet.

(2) Youth who create Internet content and use social networking sites are more likely to be targets of cyberbullying.

(3) Electronic communications provide anonymity to the perpetrator and the potential for widespread public distribution, potentially making them severely dangerous and cruel to youth.

(4) Online victimizations are associated with emotional distress and other psychological problems, including depression.

(5) Cyberbullying can cause psychological harm, including depression; negatively impact academic performance, safety, and the well-being of children in school; force children to change schools; and in some cases lead to extreme violent behavior, including murder and suicide.

(6) Sixty percent of mental health professionals who responded to the Survey of Internet Mental Health Issues report having treated at least one patient with a problematic Internet experience in the previous five years; 54 percent of these clients were 18 years of age or younger.

Source: H.R. 1966, 111th Congress, introduced April 4, 2009.

Rodney Sippel determined that school officials violated the First Amendment when they suspended a student because they found his Web site offensive. In his opinion in *Beussink v. Woodland R-IV School District*, Judge Sippel wrote: "The public interest is not only served by allowing Beussink's message to be free from censure, but also by giving the students at Woodland High School this opportunity to see the protections of the United States Constitution and the Bill of Rights at Work."[10]

Sometimes school officials need to realize that protection of student rights will serve a greater good by instructing students on the importance of constitutional freedoms. The Supreme Court said it best: "That they are educating the young for citizenship is reason for scrupulous protection of Constitutional freedoms of the individual, if we are not to strangle the free mind at its source and teach youth to discount important principles of our government as mere platitudes."[11]

Student rights are not platitudes; they are real freedoms guaranteed by the Bill of Rights in the U.S. Constitution. But while those rights must be respected, students cannot expect to exercise their rights without also showing responsibility for their own behavior.

APPENDIX ||||||▷

Beginning Legal Research

The goals of each book in the POINT/COUNTERPOINT series are not only to give the reader a basic introduction to a controversial issue affecting society, but also to encourage the reader to explore the issue more fully. This Appendix is meant to serve as a guide to the reader in researching the current state of the law as well as exploring some of the public policy arguments as to why existing laws should be changed or new laws are needed.

Although some sources of law can be found primarily in law libraries, legal research has become much faster and more accessible with the advent of the Internet. This Appendix discusses some of the best starting points for free access to laws and court decisions, but surfing the Web will uncover endless additional sources of information. Before you can research the law, however, you must have a basic understanding of the American legal system.

The most important source of law in the United States is the Constitution. Originally enacted in 1787, the Constitution outlines the structure of our federal government, as well as setting limits on the types of laws that the federal government and state governments can enact. Through the centuries, a number of amendments have added to or changed the Constitution, most notably the first 10 amendments, which collectively are known as the "Bill of Rights" and which guarantee important civil liberties.

Reading the plain text of the Constitution provides little information. For example, the Constitution prohibits "unreasonable searches and seizures" by the police. To understand concepts in the Constitution, it is necessary to look to the decisions of the U.S. Supreme Court, which has the ultimate authority in interpreting the meaning of the Constitution. For example, the U.S. Supreme Court's 2001 decision in *Kyllo v. United States* held that scanning the outside of a person's house using a heat sensor to determine whether the person is growing marijuana is an unreasonable search—if it is done without first getting a search warrant from a judge. Each state also has its own constitution and a supreme court that is the ultimate authority on its meaning.

Also important are the written laws, or "statutes," passed by the U.S. Congress and the individual state legislatures. As with constitutional provisions, the U.S. Supreme Court and the state supreme courts are the ultimate authorities in interpreting the meaning of federal and state laws, respectively. However, the U.S. Supreme Court might find that a state law violates the U.S. Constitution, and a state supreme court might find that a state law violates either the state or U.S. Constitution.

Not every controversy reaches either the U.S. Supreme Court or the state supreme courts, however. Therefore, the decisions of other courts are also important. Trial courts hear evidence from both sides and make a decision, while appeals courts review the decisions made by trial courts. Sometimes rulings from appeals courts are appealed further to the U.S. Supreme Court or the state supreme courts.

Lawyers and courts refer to statutes and court decisions through a formal system of citations. Use of these citations reveals which court made the decision or which legislature passed the statute, and allows one to quickly locate the statute or court case online or in a law library. For example, the Supreme Court case *Brown v. Board of Education* has the legal citation 347 U.S. 483 (1954). At a law library, this 1954 decision can be found on page 483 of volume 347 of the U.S. Reports, which are the official collection of the Supreme Court's decisions. On the following page, you will find samples of all the major kinds of legal citation.

Finding sources of legal information on the Internet is relatively simple thanks to "portal" sites such as findlaw.com and lexisone.com, which allow the user to access a variety of constitutions, statutes, court opinions, law review articles, news articles, and other useful sources of information. For example, findlaw.com offers access to all Supreme Court decisions since 1893. Other useful sources of information include gpo.gov, which contains a complete copy of the U.S. Code, and thomas.loc.gov, which offers access to bills pending before Congress, as well as recently passed laws. Of course, the Internet changes every second of every day, so it is best to do some independent searching.

Of course, many people still do their research at law libraries, some of which are open to the public. For example, some state governments and universities offer the public access to their law collections. Law librarians can be of great assistance, as even experienced attorneys need help with legal research from time to time.

Common Citation Forms

Source of Law	Sample Citation	Notes
U.S. Supreme Court	*Employment Division v. Smith*, 485 U.S. 660 (1988)	The U.S. Reports is the official record of Supreme Court decisions. There is also an unofficial Supreme Court ("S. Ct.") reporter.
U.S. Court of Appeals	*United States v. Lambert,* 695 F.2d 536 (11th Cir.1983)	Appellate cases appear in the Federal Reporter, designated by "F." The 11th Circuit has jurisdiction in Alabama, Florida, and Georgia.
U.S. District Court	*Carillon Importers, Ltd. v. Frank Pesce Group, Inc.,* 913 F.Supp. 1559 (S.D.Fla.1996)	Federal trial-level decisions are reported in the Federal Supplement ("F. Supp."). Some states have multiple federal districts; this case originated in the Southern District of Florida.
U.S. Code	Thomas Jefferson Commemoration Commission Act, 36 U.S.C., §149 (2002)	Sometimes the popular names of legislation—names with which the public may be familiar—are included with the U.S. Code citation.
State Supreme Court	*Sterling v. Cupp*, 290 Ore. 611, 614, 625 P.2d 123, 126 (1981)	The Oregon Supreme Court decision is reported in both the state's reporter and the Pacific regional reporter.
State Statute	Pennsylvania Abortion Control Act of 1982, 18 Pa. Cons. Stat. 3203-3220 (1990)	States use many different citation formats for their statutes.

Cases and Statutes

West Virginia State Board of Education v. Barnette, 319 U.S. 624 (1943)

The U.S. Supreme Court ruled that public school students cannot be forced to stand and salute the American flag. Such a compelled flag salute would violate the First Amendment.

Tinker v. Des Moines Independent Community School District, 393 U.S. 503 (1969)

The U.S. Supreme Court ruled that public school students do not lose their free expression rights at the schoolhouse gate. School officials cannot censor student expression unless they can reasonably forecast that the student expression will create a substantial disruption of school activities or will invade the rights of others.

Goss v. Lopez, 419 U.S. 565 (1975)

The U.S. Supreme Court ruled that public school officials must give students notice and a hearing before suspending them. The Court explained that students possess rights to procedural due process at school.

New Jersey v. T.L.O., 469 U.S. 325 (1985)

The U.S. Supreme Court ruled that public school officials did not violate the Fourth Amendment rights of a student when they searched her purse. The Court explained that the Fourth Amendment applies to public school students when searched by school officials. However, the Court ruled that public school students are not held to the high standard of probable cause when searches are being conducted.

Bethel School District No. 403 v. Fraser, 478 U.S. 675 (1986)

The U.S. Supreme Court ruled that public school officials can punish students for engaging in vulgar and lewd conduct/expression in schools. The Court explained that the purpose of education is inculcating (teaching) good values and citizenship.

Hazelwood School District v. Kuhlmeier, 484 U.S. 260 (1988)

The Supreme Court ruled that public school officials have greater control over school-sponsored student publications. If student speech is school sponsored and is not a public forum, school officials can regulate that speech if their reason for doing so is reasonably related to a legitimate educational reason.

Gun-Free Schools Act of 1994, 20 U.S.C. Chapter 70

This law says that any state that receives federal funding is required to expel from school for at least one year any student found to have brought a weapon to school.

Vernonia School District v. Acton, 515 U.S. 646 (1995)

The Supreme Court ruled that school officials can institute a random drug testing policy for high school athletes. The Court said that such a program does not violate the Fourth Amendment.

*Board of Education of Independent School District No. 92 Pottawatomie
County v. Earls,* **536 U.S. 822 (2002)**

The Supreme Court ruled that school officials can institute a random drug testing
policy of students in extracurricular activities. Relying on its earlier *Acton* decision, the Court determined that the program does not violate the Fourth Amendment.

Morse v. Frederick, **551 U.S. 393 (2007)**

The Supreme Court ruled that public school officials can punish students for
expression that the officials reasonably believe advocates illegal drug use. The case
involved a student who displayed a banner just off school grounds with the message "Bong Hits 4 Jesus."

Safford Unified School District v. Redding, **U.S. 129 S.Ct. 2633 (2009)**

The Supreme Court ruled that school officials violated the Fourth Amendment
when they subjected a student to a strip search when they had no reasonable suspicion of danger or that she was hiding contraband in her underwear. The Court
did grant the principal qualified immunity given the conflicting case law.

Terms and Concepts

Columbine

cyberbullying

disparate impact

disparate treatment

due process

equal protection clause

First Amendment

Fourteenth Amendment

Fourth Amendment

freedom of expression

individualized suspicion

in loco parentis

probable cause

reasonable suspicion

substantive due process

Title VI of the Civil Rights Act of 1964

zero tolerance

Introduction: Constitutional Rights in School

1. *West Virginia State Board of Education v. Barnette*, 319 U.S. 624, 637 (1943).

2 Stuart Levitan, "Is Anyone Listening to Our Students? A Plea for Respect and Inclusion," *Florida State University Law Review* 21 (1993): pp. 35, 40.

3 *Tinker v. Des Moines Independent Community School District*, 393 U.S. 503, 511 (1969).

4 David L. Hudson Jr., "On 30-Year Anniversary, *Tinker* Participants Look Back at Landmark Case," February 24, 1999, First Amendment Center. http://www. firstamendmentcenter.org/analysis. aspx?id=5582.

5 David Hudson, "Free-speech Experts Describe Texas Student-rights Case as '*Tinker* Revisited'," July 23, 1999, First Amendment Center. http://www. firstamendmentcenter.org/news. aspx?id=7859.

6 "ACLU Challenges Louisiana School's Ban on Armbands," ACLU News Release, November 1, 1999. http://www. aclu.org/free-speech/aclu-challenges-louisiana-schools-ban-armbands-viola-tion-students first amendment rights.

7 *Lowry v. Watson Chapel School District*, 540 F.3d 752 (8th Cir. 2008).

Point: Zero Tolerance Policies Work

1 Remarks by the President Clinton to the Students of Carlmont High School and in Signing the Presidential Memorandum: "Zero Tolerance for Guns in Schools," October 22, 1994. http://www. ed.gov/PressReleases/10-1994/guns. html.

2 Paul M. Bogos, "Expelled. No Excuses, No Exceptions." Michigan's Zero Tolerance Policy in Response to School Violence," M.C.L.A. Section 380.1311, *University of Detroit Law Review* 74 (1997): p. 357.

3 *New Jersey v. T.L.O.*, 469 U.S. 325, 339 (1985).

4 LA R.S. 17 § 416.15 (2001).

5 Carol Silverman Saunders, *Safe at School: Awareness and Action for Parents.* New York: St. Martin's, 1999, p. 51.

6 Ruth Zweifler and Julia De Beers, "The Children Left Behind: How Zero Tolerance Impacts Our Most Vulnerable Youth," *Michigan Journal of Race and Law* 8 (2002): pp. 191, 195.

7 "Zero Tolerance Restores Peace to Middle School," *School Violence Alert*, Vol. 1, No. 10 (October 1995).

8 School Safety Study, National Association of Elementary School Principals 1997 National Poll.

9 School Safety Study, "1997: Gallup Organization and Phi Delta Kappan."

10 Sandra Feldman, "Let's Stay the Course," American Federation of Teachers (February 2000).

11 Del Stover, "Despite Charges of Unfairness, Zero Tolerance is Working," *School Board News*, January 2000.

12 Clinton, Zero Tolerance Remarks.

13 No. 00-2157 (4th Cir.)(July 30, 2001).

14 Ibid., p. 2.

15 *Cathe A. v. Doddridge County Board. of Education*, 490 S.E.2d 340 (W.V. 1997).

16 *S.G. v. Sayreville Board of Education*, 333 F.3d 417, 425 (3rd Cir. 2003).

17 *Anderson v. Milbank School District*, 197 F.R.D. 682 (D.S.D. 2000).

18 *South Gibson School Board v. Sollman*, 768 N.E.2d 316, 441 (Ind. 2002).

19 Roger W. Ashford, "Can Zero-Tolerance Keep Our Schools Safe," *NASP Communique*. Vol. 29: #8.

Counterpoint: Zero Tolerance Policies Are Unfair

1 Russell Skiba and Kimberly Knesting, "Zero Tolerance, Zero Evidence: An Analysis of School Disciplinary Practice," *Zero Tolerance: Can Suspension and Expulsion Keep Schools Safe?*, eds. Russell J. Skiba and Gil G. Noam. San Francisco: Jossey-Bass, 2001: pp. 17, 22.

2 J. Kevin Jenkins and John Dayton, "Students, Weapons, and Due Process: An Analysis of Zero Tolerance Policies in Public Schools," *Education Law Reporter* 171 (2003): pp. 13, 33.

3 Judith A. Browne, Daniel J. Losen, and Johanna Wald, "Zero Tolerance: Unfair, with Little Recourse," *Zero Tolerance: Can Suspension and Expulsion Keep Schools Safe?* eds. Russell J. Skiba and Gil G. Noam. San Francisco: Jossey-Bass, 2001: p. 73.

4 American Bar Association Zero Toler-ance Resolution. http://www.abanet.org/crimjust/juvjus/zerotolres.html.
5 Skiba and Knesting, p. 35.
6 Ronnie Casella, *At Zero Tolerance: Punishment, Prevention, and School Violence.* New York: Peter Lang Publishing, Inc., 2001, p. 175.
7 Skiba and Knesting, pp. 36–37.
8 Browne, Losen, and Wald, p. 74.
9 Rebecca Gordon, Libero Della Piana, and Terry Keleher, "Zero Tolerance: A Basic Racial Report Card," *Zero Tolerance*, eds. William Ayers, Bernardine Dohrn, and Rick Ayers. New York: The New Press, 2001, p. 165.
10 "Opportunities Suspended: The Devastating Consequences of Zero Tolerance and School Discipline," The Advancement Project/Civil Rights Project, (June 2000).
11 *Goss v. Lopez*, 419 U.S. 565 (1975).
12 Ibid., p. 578.
13 *Lyons v. Penn Hills School District*, 723 A.2d 1073, 1076 (Pa. Commonwealth Ct. 1999).
14 *Seal v. Morgan*, 229 F.3d 567, 575 (6th Cir. 2000).
15 Ibid., p. 578.
16 Ibid., p. 579.
17 Ibid., p. 581.
18 *Colvin v. Lowndes County*, 114 F. Supp.2d 504, 513 (N.D. Miss. 1999).

Point: Safety Concerns Must Trump Fourth Amendment Rights in Public Schools

1 Mary Ellen O'Toole, *The School Shooter: A Threat Assessment Perspective.* Federal Bureau of Investigation, 1999. http://www.fbi.gov/publications/school/school2.pdf.
2 Darcia Harris Bowman and Michelle Galley, "As Alert Issued, Schools Urged to Review Security." *Education Week*, February 19, 2003: p. 1.
3 "Violent Behavior of Youth on Rise."
4 20 U.S.C. 8921.
5 *New Jersey v. T.L.O.*, 469 U.S. 325, 342 (1985).
6 Ibid., p. 343.
7 *Vernonia School District v. Acton*, 515 U.S. 646 (1995).

8 *Board of Education of Independent School District No. 92 of Pottawatomie County v. Earls*, 536 U.S. 822 (2002).
9 *Vernonia*, 515 U.S., p. 657.
10 Ibid., p. 662.
11 Ibid., pp. 664–665.
12 *Board of Education of Independent School District No. 92 of Pottawatomie County v. Earls*, 536 U.S. 822, 830 (2002).
13 *In Re F.B.*, 726 A.2d 361 (Pa. 1999).
14 Ibid., p. 366.
15 Sanders, *Safe At School*, p. 49.
16 See *In Re Patrick Y.*, 746 A.2d 405 (Md. App. 2001); *In Re Isiah B.*, 500 N.W.2d 637 (Wis. 1993); *Shoemaker v. State*, 971 S.W.2d 178 (Tex. App. 1998).

Counterpoint: Students Must Not Lose Their Fourth Amendment Rights

1 *New Jersey v. T.L.O.*, 469 U.S. 325, 342 (1985).
2 Ibid., p. 385 (J. Stevens, dissenting).
3 *Vernonia School District v. Acton*, 515 U.S.: 646, 667 (J. O'Connor, dissenting).
4 Ibid., p. 680 (J. O'Connor, dissenting).
5 *Board of Education v. Earls*, 536 U.S. 822, 843 (J. Ginsburg, dissenting).
6 Ralph D. Mawdsley and Charles J. Russo, *Drug Testing for School Extracurricular Activities*, 173 Education Law Reporter (2003): pp. 1, 15.
7 Nathan L. Essex, *School Law and the Public Schools: A Practical Guide for Educational Leaders*, 2nd ed. Boston: Allyn & Bacon, 2002, p. 73.
8 *Bell v. Marseilles Elementary School*, 160 F.Supp.2d 883, 889 (E.D. Ill. 2001).
9 *Safford Unified School District v. Redding*, 129 S.Ct. 2633, 2643 (2009).
10 *Kennedy v. Dexter Consolidated Schools*, 10 P.3d 115, 122 (N.M. 2000)
11 Ibid., p. 121.
12 *Fewless v. Board of Education of Wayland Union Schools*, 208 F.Supp.2d 806, 819 (W.D. Mich. 2002).
13 Dean Schabner, "Trust Betrayed? School Security Tapes of Kids Undressing Viewed on Net, Suit Says," ABCNews.com, July 16, 2003.
14 *New Jersey v. T.L.O.*, 469 U.S., pp. 338–339.

15 Crystal A. Garcia and Sheila Suess Kennedy, "Back to School: Technology, School Safety and the Disappearing Fourth Amendment," 12 *Kansas Journal of Law and Public Policy* (2003): pp. 273, 280.

16 *New Jersey v. T.L.O.*, 469 U.S., at 339.

17 *In Re Interest of S.C.*, 583 So.2d 188 (Miss. 1991); *State v. Jones*, 666 N.W.2d 142 (Iowa 2003).

18 Essex, p. 71.

Point: School Dress Codes Are Constitutional

1 Todd DeMitchell, Richard Fossey, and Casey Cobb. "Dress Codes in the Public Schools: Principals, Policies and Precepts," 29 *Journal of Law and Education* (2000): pp. 31, 45.

2 National Association of Elementary School Principals, "Information and Resources: Public School Uniforms."

3 President Bill Clinton, State of the Union Address, January 23, 1996.

4 Alison Mitchell, "Clinton Will Advise Schools on Uniforms," *New York Times*, February 25, 1996, p. 1.

5 Department of Education, "Manual on School Uniforms." http://www2.ed.gov/updates/uniforms.html.

6 Saunders, *Safe At School: Awareness and Action for Parents.*

7 Kerry A. White, "Do School Uniforms Fit?" *School Administrator* (February 2000).

8 *Spence v. Washington*, 418 U.S. 405 (1974).

9 *Tinker v. Des Moines Independent Community School District*, 393 U.S. 503 (1969).

10 *Bethel School District v. Fraser*, 478 U.S. 675 (1986).

11 *Hazelwood School District v. Kuhlmeier*, 484 U.S. 260 (1988).

12 *Morse v. Frederick*, 551 U.S. 393 (2007).

13 *Fraser*, 478 U.S. 681.

14 *Broussard v. School Board of Norfolk*, 801 F.Supp. 1526 (E.D. Va. 1992).

15 *Morse*, 551 U.S. 403.

16 *Bivens v. Albuquerque Public Schools*, 899 F. Supp. 556 (D. N.M. 1995).

17 *Littlefield v. Forney Independent School District*, 268 F.3d 275 (5th Cir. 2001).

18 Ibid., p. 287.

19 Ibid., p. 291.

20 *Canady v. Bossier Parish School Board*, 240 F.3d 437 (5th Cir. 2001).

21 *Canady*, 240 F.3d, p. 443; *Littlefield*, 268 F.3d, p. 286.

Counterpoint: School Dress Codes Are Unconstitutional

1 Loren Siegel, "Point of View: School Uniforms," March 1, 1996.

2 Wendell Anderson, "School Dress Codes and Uniform Policies," *Policy Report, ERIC Clearinghouse on Educational Policy and Management*, University of Oregon (Fall 2002), p. 7.

3 Alison Barbarosh, "Undressing the First Amendment in Public Schools: Do Uniform Dress Codes Violate Students' First Amendment Rights?" 28 *Loyola of Los Angeles Law Review* (1995): pp. 1415, 1445–1446.

4 David L. Brunsma and Kerry A. Rockquemore, "The Effects of Student Uniforms on Attendance, Behavior Problems, Substance Use, and Academic Achievement," *Journal of Educational Research* (September-October 1998).

5 Amy Mitchell Watson, "Public School Dress Codes: The Constitutional Debate," *Brigham Young University Education and Law Journal* (1998): pp. 147, 148.

6 *Melton v. Young*, 465 F.2d 1322 (6th Cir. 1972); *West v. Derby Unified School District*, 206 F.3d 1358 (10th Cir. 2000).

7 *Castorina v. Madison County School Board*, 246 F.3d 536, 541 (6th Cir. 2001).

8 *Jeglin v. San Jacinto Unified School District*, 827 F.Supp. 1459 (C.D. Cal. 1993).

9 *Scott v. Napa Valley Unified School District*, No. 26-370862 (Cal. Superior Court)(7/2/2007), at p. 7, http://www.aclunc.org/docs/Freedom_of_press_and_speech/Opinion_and_Order_Granting_Preliminary_Injunction.pdf.

10 Associated Press, "Calif. School District Loosens Dress Code that Banned Tigger," August 13, 2007, First Amendment

Center. http://www.firstamendment center.org/news.aspx?id=18912.

11 *Adams v. Township of Redford*, 1996 WL 250578 (No. 95-1279) (May 10, 1996).

12 *McIntire v. Bethel School Independent School District*, 804 F.Supp. 1415, 1420 (W.D. Okl. 1992).

13 *Hicks v. Halifax County Board of Education*, 93 F.Supp. 2d 649 (E.D. N.C. 1999).

14 "Student, N.C. School District Settle Lawsuit Over Uniforms," Freedom Forum Online, (January 12, 2000). http://www.freedom-forum.org/templates/document. asp?documentID=8816.

15 Associated Press, "Federal Judge: Uniforms May Stay, But So May Student's Armband," November 28, 1999, First Amendment Center. http://www. firstamendmentcenter.org/news. aspx?id=8289.

16 *Pierce v. Society of Sisters,* 268 U.S. 510, 534–535 (1925).

17 David L. Hudson Jr., "Parents Across the South Battle Mandatory School Dress Codes," August 17, 1999, First Amendment Center. http://www.first amendmentcenter.org/news.aspx?id =7810.

18 Ibid.

19 Essex, *School Law and the Public Schools*, pp. 57–58.

Conclusion: The Future of Student Rights

1 Nadine Strossen, "Students' Rights and How They Are Wronged," 32 *University of Richmond Law Review* (1998): pp. 457, 458.

2 David L. Hudson Jr. and John E. Ferguson Jr., "The Courts' Inconsistent Treatment of *Bethel v. Fraser* and the Curtailment of Student Rights," 36 *John Marshall Law Review*. (2002): pp. 181, 190.

3 David L. Hudson Jr., "Overview: K–12 Public School Student Expression," First Amendment Center. http://www.firsta-mendmentcenter.org/Speech/studentex-pression/overview.aspx.

4 David L. Hudson Jr., "Student Online Expression: What Do the Internet and MySpace Mean for Students' First Amendment Rights?" December 2006, First Amendment Center. http://www. firstamendmentcenter.org/PDF/student. internet.speech.pdf.

5 Nancy Willard, "Student Online Speech and the Boundaries of the Schoolhouse Gate," March 31, 2009, First Amendment Center, http://www. firstamendmentcenter.org/analysis. aspx?id=21423.

6 Ibid.

7 Ibid.

8 H.R. 1966, the Megan Meier Cyberbullying Prevention Act. (111th Congress).

9 Stuart Leviton, "Is Anyone Listening To Our Students? A Plea for Respect and Inclusion," 21 *Florida State University Law Review* (1993): pp. 35, 40, 74.

10 *Beussink v. Woodland R-IV School District*, 30 F.Supp. 2d 1175, 1182 (E.D.M. 1998).

11 *West Virginia State Board of Education v. Barnette*, 319 U.S. 624, 637 (1943).

Books and Articles

Anderson, Wendell. "School Dress Codes and Uniform Policies." *Policy Report, ERIC Clearinghouse on Educational Policy and Management*, University of Oregon (Fall 2002). Available online. URL: http://eric.uoregon.edu/publications/policy_reports/dress_codes/intro.html.

Ayers, William, Rick Ayers, and Bernardine Dohrn, eds. *Zero Tolerance: Resisting the Drive for Punishment in our Schools.* New York: The New Press, 2001.

Barbarosh, Alison M. "Undressing the First Amendment in Public Schools: Do Uniform Dress Codes Violate Students' First Amendment Rights?" *Loyola of Los Angeles Law Review* 28 (1995): p. 1415.

Bogos, Paul M. "Expelled. No Excuses, No Exceptions." Michigan's Zero Tolerance Policy in Response to School Violence. M.C.L.A. Section 380.1311. *University of Detroit Mercy Law Review* 74 (1997): p. 357.

Brunsma, David, and Kerry A. Rockquemore. "The Effects of Student Uniforms on Attendance, Behavior Problems, Substance Use, and Academic Achievement." *Journal of Educational Research* (September–October 1998).

Calvert, Clay. "Free Speech and Public Schools in a Post-Columbine World: Check Your Speech Rights at the Schoolhouse Metal Detector." *University of Denver Law Review* 77 (2000): p. 739.

Cambron-McCabe, Nelda H., Stephen B. Thomas, and Martha M. McCarthy. *Public School Law: Teacher's and Student's Rights*, 5th ed. New York: Allyn & Bacon, 2003.

Cary, Eve, Alan H. Levine, and Janet Price. *The Rights of Students: ACLU Handbook for Young Americans.* New York: Puffin, 1997.

Casella, Ronnie. *At Zero Tolerance: Punishment, Prevention, and School Violence.* New York: Peter Lang Publishing, 2001.

Chemerinsky, Erwin. "Students Do Leave Their First Amendment Rights at the Schoolhouse Gates: What's Left of *Tinker*?" *Drake Law Review* 48 (2000): p. 527.

Cordero, Rebecca N. "No Expectation of Privacy: Should School Officials Be Able to Search Students' Lockers Without Any Suspicion of Wrongdoing? A Study of *In Re Patrick Y.* and Its Effect on Maryland Public School Students," *University of Baltimore Law Review* 31(2002): p. 305.

DeMitchell, Todd A., Richard Fossey, and Casey Cobb. "Dress Codes in the Public Schools: Principals, Policies and Precepts." *Journal of Law and Education* 21 (2000): p. 31.

Dupre, Anne Proffitt. *Speaking Up: The Unintended Costs of Free Speech in Public Schools.* Boston: Harvard University Press, 2009.

Essex, Nathan L. *School Law and the Public Schools: A Practical Guide for Educational Leaders,* 2nd ed. Boston: Allyn and Bacon, 2002.

———. *A Teacher's Pocket Guide to School Law.* Boston: Pearson Education, 2006.

Garcia, Crystal A., and Sheila Suess Kennedy. "Back to School: Technology, School Safety and the Disappearing Fourth Amendment." *Kansas Journal of Law and Public Policy* 12 (Winter 2003): p. 273.

Henault, Cherry. "Zero Tolerance in Schools." *Journal of Law and Education* 30 (July 2001): p. 547.

Hudson, David L., Jr. "Censorship of Student Internet Speech: The Effect of Diminishing Student Rights, Fear of the Internet and Columbine." *Michigan State University Law Review* (2000): p. 199. Available online. URL: http://www.freedomforum.org/templates/document. asp?documentID=14592.

———. "Fear of Violence In Our Schools: Is 'Undifferentiated Fear' in the Age of Columbine Leading to a Suppression of Student Speech?" *Washburn Law Journal* 42 (2002). Available online. URL: http://washburnlaw. edu/wlj/42-1/articles/hudson-david.pdf.

———. "Student Online Expression: What Do the Internet and MySpace Mean for Students' First Amendment Rights?" First Amendment Center, December 2006. Available online. URL: http://www. firstamendmentcenter.org/about.aspx?id=17913.

———, and John E. Ferguson Jr. "The Courts' Inconsistent Treatment of Bethel v. Fraser and the Curtailment of Student Rights." *John Marshall Law Review* 36 (2002): p. 181.

Irons, Peter, ed. *May It Please the Court: Courts, Kids, and the Constitution.* New York: The New Press, 2000.

Jenkins, J. Kevin, and John Dayton. "Students, Weapons, and Due Process: An Analysis of Zero Tolerance Policies in Public Schools." *Education Law Reporter* 171 (January 2, 2003): p. 13.

Johnson, John W. *The Struggle for Student Rights:* Tinker v. Des Moines *and the 1960s.* Lawrence: University Press of Kansas, 1997.

Levitan, Stuart. "Is Anyone Listening To Our Students? A Plea for Respect and Inclusion," *Florida State University Law Review* 21 (1993): p. 35.

Mahling, Wendy. "Secondhand Codes: An Analysis of the Constitutionality of Dress Codes in the Public Schools." *Minnesota Law Review* 80 (1996): p. 715.

Mawdsley, Ralph D., and Charles J. Russo. "Drug Testing for School Extra-curricular Activities." *Education Law Reporter* 173 (March 13, 2003): p. 1.

McManimon, Shannon. "Say What?: High School Students' Rights." Y & M Online (October 2000).

Monk, Linda R. *The Bill of Rights: A User's Guide.* Washington, D.C.: Close Up Publishing, 1995.

———. *The Words We Live By: Your Annotated Guide to the Constitution.* New York: Hyperion Press, 2003.

"Opportunities Suspended: The Devastating Consequences of Zero Tolerance and School Discipline Policies." The Advancement Project/Civil Rights Project, (June 2000).

Penrose, Meg. "Shedding Rights, Shredding Rights: A Critical Examination of Students' Privacy Rights and the 'Special Needs' Doctrine After *Earls*," *Nevada Law Journal* 3 (2003): p. 411.

Raskin, Jamin B. *We the Students: Supreme Court Cases For and About Students.* Washington, D.C.: Congressional Quarterly Books, 2003.

———. "No Enclaves of Totalitarianism: The Triumph and Unrealized Promise of the *Tinker* Decision." *American Law Review* 58 (2009): p. 1193.

Royal, Ashley C. "Expanding the Scope of Suspicionless Drug Testing in Public Schools." *Mercer Law Review* 54 (2003): p. 1293.

Sarke, Dena M. "Coed Naked Constitutional Law: The Benefits and Harms of Uniform Dress Requirements in American Public Schools." *Boston University Law Review* 78 (1998): p. 153.

Sprow, Michael A. "The High Price of Safety: May Public Schools Institute a Policy of Frisking Students as They Enter the Building?" *Baylor Law Review* 54 (2002): p. 133.

Strossen, Nadine. "Students' Rights and How They are Wronged." *University of Richmond Law Review* 32 (1998): p. 457.

Thomas, Garth. "Random Suspicionless Drug Testing: Are Students No Longer Afforded Fourth Amendment Protections?" *New York Law School Journal of Human Rights* (2003): p. 451.

Tinker, Mary Beth. "Reflections on Tinker." *American University Law Review* 58 (2009): p. 1119.

U.S. Department of Education's Manual on School Uniforms. Available online. URL: http://www.ed.gov/updates/uniforms.html.

White, Kerry A. "Do School Uniforms Fit?" *School Administrator* (February 2000).

Wilson, Amy Mitchell. "Public School Dress Codes: The Constitutional Debate." *Brigham Young University Education and Law Journal* (1998): p. 147.

Yearout, Jason E. "Individualized School Searches and the Fourth Amendment: What's A School District To Do?" *College of William and Mary Law School* 10 (2002): p. 489.

Zweifler, Ruth, and Julia De Beers. "The Children Left Behind: How Zero Tolerance Impacts Our Most Vulnerable Youth." *The Michigan Journal of Race and Law* 8 (2002): p. 191.

Web Sites
American Center for Law and Justice
http://www.aclj.org/
This advocacy group deals with the religious liberty rights of students. It deals with student rights such as Bible clubs, clothing, prayer, religious displays, and witnessing.

American Civil Liberties Union—Student Rights

http://www.aclu.org/about-aclu-0

This civil liberties organization has a section on its Web site devoted to the subject of student rights. It includes discussions on dress codes and uniforms, drug testing, due process/zero tolerance, freedom of expression, and other topics.

American Federation of Teachers

http://www.aft.org/

This organization examines pressing issues facing teachers in K–12 and higher education. The site contains a wealth of information on a variety of school law topics.

The First Amendment Center Online

http://www.firstamendmentcenter.org

The First Amendment Center, a nonprofit organization devoted to bringing greater public awareness and appreciation of the First Amendment, has a Web site with good overviews of free expression topics, including free expression and religious liberty in the public schools.

Kidspeak!

http://www.kidspeakonline.org

This group deals with kids "speaking up for free speech." It talks about various censorship issues facing children in schools and libraries.

National Association of Elementary School Principals

http://www.naesp.org/

This group serves all elementary and middle school principals. Its Web site contains useful discussions of many school law issues.

National Association of State Boards of Education

http://www.nasbe.org/

This nonprofit organization helps school board leaders set policy and improve education. Its Web site contains a section entitled "Education Issues."

National Coalition Against Censorship

http://www.ncac.org/

This civil liberties group opposes different forms of government censorship. Its Web site contains useful information regarding censorship in public schools.

National School Boards Association

http://www.nsba.org

This organization represents those who govern public schools. Its Web site contains a section on school law. Many other resources are included.

The Rutherford Institute

http://www.rutherford.org/

This civil liberties group, which often protects the religious liberty rights of students, has a Web site with sections on zero tolerance, free speech, religious freedom, parents' rights, and other issues.

Student Press Law Center

http://www.splc.org

This excellent Web site contains detailed information about students' free press rights. The SPLC advocates on behalf of students who feel they have been censored unfairly by school administrators.

PICTURE CREDITS

Page numbers in *italics* indicate photos or illustrations.

CONTRIBUTORS ////▷

DAVID L. HUDSON JR. is a First Amendment Scholar at the First Amendment Center at Vanderbilt University. He teaches law classes at Middle Tennessee State University, Nashville School of Law, and Vanderbilt Law School. He is the author or coauthor of more than 20 books, including several in the POINT/COUNTERPOINT series.

ALAN MARZILLI, M.A., J.D., lives in Birmingham, Ala., and is a program associate with Advocates for Human Potential, Inc., a research and consulting firm based in Sudbury, Mass., and Albany, N.Y. He primarily works on developing training and educational materials for agencies of the federal government on topics such as housing, mental health policy, employment, and transportation. He has spoken on mental health issues in 30 states, the District of Columbia, and Puerto Rico; his work has included training mental health administrators, nonprofit management and staff, and people with mental illnesses and their families on a wide variety of topics, including effective advocacy, community-based mental health services, and housing. He has written several handbooks and training curricula that are used nationally and as far away as the territory of Guam. He managed statewide and national mental health advocacy programs and worked for several public interest lobbying organizations while studying law at Georgetown University. He has written more than a dozen books, including numerous titles in the POINT/COUNTERPOINT series.